Ring by Spring

Ring by Spring

DATING AND RELATIONSHIP CULTURES
AT CHRISTIAN COLLEGES

Stacy Keogh George

 CASCADE *Books* • Eugene, Oregon

RING BY SPRING
Dating and Relationship Cultures at Christian Colleges

Cascade Books
An Imprint of Wipf and Stock Publishers
199 W. 8th Ave., Suite 3
Eugene, OR 97401

www.wipfandstock.com

PAPERBACK ISBN: 978-1-5326-3562-5
HARDCOVER ISBN: 978-1-5326-3564-9
EBOOK ISBN: 978-1-5326-3563-2

Cataloguing-in-Publication data:

Names: George, Stacy Keogh, author.

Title: Ring by spring : dating and relationship cultures at Christian colleges / by Stacy Keogh George.

Description: Eugene, OR: Cascade Books, 2019 | Includes bibliographical references.

Identifiers: ISBN 978-1-5326-3562-5 (paperback) | ISBN 978-1-5326-3564-9 (hardcover) | ISBN 978-1-5326-3563-2 (ebook)

Subjects: LCSH: Dating (Social customs)—Religious aspects—Christianity. | Courtship—Religious aspects—Christianity. | Universities and colleges—Social aspects—United States.

Classification: BV4597.53.M36 G46 2019 (print) | BV4597.53.M36 (ebook)

Manufactured in the U.S.A.   JULY 24, 2019

Dedication

For my students who need to be heard and healed.
For my colleagues who nurture the brave spaces to have
courageous conversations.
For my boys, for whom I pray always
have freedom in life and love.

CONTENTS

List of Tables and Figures ix

Preface xi

Acknowledgments xvi

Chapter 1 — Introduction 1

Chapter 2 — Christian Colleges 11

Chapter 3 — Setting the Scene 25

Chapter 4 — Gendered Norms 41

Chapter 5 — Sex and Sexuality 57

Chapter 6 — Interpretations and Impact 73

Chapter 7 — Equipped 88

Epilogue 101

Discussion Questions 103

Bibliography 109

LIST OF TABLES
AND FIGURES

Table 3.1 Christian College Newspaper Depictions of Ring by Spring

Table 3.2 Source of Pressure by Graduating Cohort

Table 3.3 Perspectives on Dating

Table 3.4 Pressure to Marry and Church Attendance

Table 3.5 Relationship Status upon Graduation

Table 3.6 Marital Status upon Graduation by Gender

Table 4.1 Pressure to Marry by Gender

Table 5.1 Church Attendance and Sexual Activity

Table 5.2 LGBT Students and Pressure to Marry During College

Figure 2.1 Average Age of Marriage in the US (1960–2010)

Figure 3.1 Pressure to Marry During College

Figure 7.1 Percentage of Engaged Students Feeling Prepared to Marry

PREFACE

I DID NOT REALIZE it at the time, but my research on *Ring by Spring* began fifteen years before I started collecting data for this project. My first exposure to the dating world at Christian colleges began when I was a teenager. I was very active in the high school youth group at my church and saw many of the graduating high school seniors continue at Christian colleges. They would come home on holiday breaks with their girlfriends or boyfriends, and would share with the entire congregation the news of their recent engagements or plans to become engaged. Most of the young adults from my youth group attended one specific Christian college in my home state, so I assumed that this culture of finding a mate during college was something that this particular school encouraged, or at least impressed upon its student population. In preparation for college, therefore, our youth leaders spent quite a bit of time talking about relationships and sex from "the Christian perspective." As I learned more about purity culture and the courtship process, I became confused about how I was supposed to find a spouse without dating, which seemed contrary to the experiences of everyone I knew outside of my Christian circles, or even in my own family. Nonetheless, my parents were clear that we should not get married before we finished college, so I knew that my college experience would focus primarily on earning my degree.

I chose to attend a small Christian liberal arts university in the northwestern United States, deviating from the norm of my youth group. Though I was already somewhat familiar with Christian college culture, the enormous pressure nonetheless overwhelmed me. I immediately felt that I needed to succeed not only in achieving a college degree, but to leave college with an engagement ring on my finger. The staff or faculty with whom I interacted did not impose this pressure on me. It came from my peers: my hall mates in the dormitory, young women in my freshman seminar course, conversations I had during Bible study small groups on campus. Not a month into my first year I started seeing bridal magazines appear in the dorm bathrooms and common areas. I began to notice the awkward flirtations and stifled relationships between young men and women all around campus. The interactions were not as casual as the ones I had witnessed and participated in at my public high school. Even same-sex friendships in my friend group struggled to survive amidst the mounting competition to win the most eligible bachelor on campus.

These musings did not end with the "freshmen frenzy"—the rush to partner up before all the "desirable" men and women were taken. I recall a conversation my sophomore year that began as harmless chatter about dating but turned into a group bet on who would get married first out of our group of four. I was voted last by the others. Admittedly, I had expressed zero interest in marrying any of the men at my college, and I already committed to study abroad the following academic year. I did want to marry eventually, but my sights were set on my career post-graduation, making that a priority over marriage at the time. Still, the conversation left me feeling unworthy and hopeless. Never mind that my friends were right: I did not marry until I was thirty-two, and I still consider waiting to be one of the best decisions of my life. Still, the impact of that conversation, perpetuated by the expectation to marry from everyone else on my campus, made me feel insecure about my life choices and my value as a woman.

I love weddings. Most people are happy, and the guests get to celebrate the union of two amazing people (presumably, you think they are amazing if you took the time and effort to attend and buy them a gift). During college and immediately after I participated in quite a few weddings, both as a member of the bridal party and as a guest. At the time, I trusted the decisions my friends made and believe that they made the right choice for themselves. While I am not privy to the internal dynamics of the marriages, I continue to believe that their love story started in the right place at the right time. However, I also have acquaintances from college whose marriages that started at age twenty-two ended shortly after they began.

While all of these relationship status changes were happening with my peers, I took advantage of my singlehood, traveled the world, and established the career that I dreamt of, all the while dating some interesting men and learning a lot about life in the process. My love story was very different from the ring by spring couples of my early adulthood. I met my now-husband when I was twenty-nine, two weeks after I successfully defended my doctoral dissertation, and the same weekend I accepted my first tenure-track job. My love story is just as amazing as the stories of my friends from college, and it most certainly came at the right place at the right time. I was also content—even happy—being a single professional with the world at my fingertips. I am thrilled I met my husband, but I did not feel that I had to marry him to be complete.

When I returned to Christian higher education as a professor in 2013, I was shocked to hear that the ring by spring culture still pervaded student life. Within the first month of the first semester teaching on my new campus, I had three female students mention their concerns about leaving college unengaged, or unwilling to make a lifetime commitment to their boyfriend in the upcoming year. Perhaps they approached me because I was a new female faculty member—the only female faculty member!—in the department. On the other hand, perhaps they approached me because they saw me as a single (at the time) woman who was self-sufficient and clearly content with her life choices. I wondered how many mentors they had encountered who encouraged them to pursue their vocations, rather than pressuring them to find a husband to fulfill the expectations of others. Being a sociologist, I developed a research plan to understand this not-so-hidden culture on Christian college campuses.

Despite my best attempts to remain objective throughout the course of this research, I find it difficult to detach entirely from the impact of the dating culture on my personal life and the lives of some of my classmates. I hope and pray that the stories told throughout this book demonstrate the complexity of the ring by spring culture, while also celebrating the variety of ways in which Christian students experience relationships, be it as a single, coupled, engaged, or married person.

The purpose of this book is not to condemn Christian college marriages, or even to dismantle them—though I will leave it up to the reader to use judgement on the value that the ring by spring tradition provides to a campus community. Instead, I hope to encourage readers to develop a deeper understanding of how the pressure to marry impacts Christian college students. I focus primarily on the influences and sociological dynamics that lead Christian young adults (mostly young women) to feel the need to marry upon graduation. Each chapter begins with a personal reflection from a Christian college graduate who was in some way impacted by ring by spring during his or her college years. I hope that individuals associated with Christian institutions—be it professionals in higher education, churches, organizations, or students and other participants in these establishments—grasp the gravity of the impact of ring by spring on singleness, dating, and marriage on Christian college campuses. The evidence suggests that while ring by spring has had a negative impact on some students, that does not suggest that all students have been equally distressed by its presence on campus. For those students who meet their match in college, let us celebrate and support them in their journey. However, for those who remain single upon graduation, investigating this culture in more detail may teach us how to approach conversations about dating and marriage with delicacy.

This book is for everyone: academics and nonacademics, Christians and non-Christians, and academics interested in variable dating and marriage patterns evident in the contemporary United States. I have structured the book in an intentionally concise and approachable format, so that it does not exclude readers from outside the field of sociology, or those outside of academia in general. While I do rely on biblical passages and Christian theology to inform this work, it does not need to be read from strictly a Christian perspective. My hope is that administrators, faculty, and staff working at colleges in North America will use this as a tool for recognizing the impact of dating culture on their campuses. Many of us are in direct contact with this culture, and by exposing readers to some of the internal dynamics, perhaps we will be better prepared to equip our students for life beyond college.

This book may also be preparation material for high school juniors and seniors, or college freshman to prepare them for the nonconventional dating rituals that appear on Christian college campuses. Consequently, I have included a list of discussion questions at the end as a starting point for students to begin thinking critically about their dating experiences on campuses.

In the end, however, this book is for Christian college students, past and present. It is not meant to be prescriptive, but rather descriptive of the impact ring by spring has on young Christian adults. I embarked on this project with the intention of sharing stories from students who were single, coupled, and married, so that students may recognize that there are many paths to satisfaction, and that, ultimately, one's worth is not hinged on a person's relationship status. I hope that they may discover redemption by reading through the stories recounted throughout the chapters that follow.

ACKNOWLEDGMENTS

THE PAST FIVE YEARS I have spent researching this topic could not have been possible without the overwhelming encouragement and support of my students, colleagues, friends, and family.

The stories that unfold in this manuscript reflect the bravery of the Christian college students that guided this project. I am so grateful for the students—past and present—who were bold enough to share their experiences and expose their vulnerabilities to shed light on this important topic. This is your story. I thank you for entrusting me to synthesize your experiences so that we may all be aware of the impact ring by spring has had on your lives. I am particularly grateful for those students who shall remain anonymous who participated in the focus groups: You are all amazing individuals whose convictions, courage, and openness is admirable. I also want to thank Melia Deters, Sarah Dixit, Sonia Klouse, Margot Spindola, and Emily Moline Meyers for working with me in the early stages of analysis. Their research appears in various ways throughout the book.

My friends and colleagues at Whitworth University have not only expressed interest in this research, but provided me with resources to complete the project. I am continually impressed by your own research, and am thankful for your time to help me review and refine this quasi-sociological study. To the Department of Sociology—Jason Wollschleger, Mark Killian, Jacquie van Wormer, and Martin Hughes—thank you for the opportunity to workshop the paper, and helping me refine my outline. To the Office of Academic Affairs and the Faculty Research and Development committee for the resources to allow me to finish this project in a timely fashion. To Stephanee Newman and Elise Kemp for nitpicking the first draft of the manuscript. To Doug Jones, Mindy Smith, and Nicole Sheets for sharing your ideas with me over coffee or over email. I also want to thank my pastor and friend, Eric Peterson, for letting me use your book as my guide, for your theological insight, and your reassurance of the value of this study.

This project could not have covered so many topical areas if not for the Christian college alum that participated in the surveys. Thanks to my friends who helped spread the survey so that we captured the voices of Christian college alumni around the country.

I can't express enough gratitude for the support from my loving and very patient family. Bart, thanks for "grading" my early drafts, and for listening to me process ideas even when you had no idea what I was talking about. Thank you for the sacrifices you made to our family to allow me time to finish this project. And to my baby boy, Everett, who was my inspiration to write this even before he was born. I could not have done this project without their cheers from the sidelines.

Finally, I thank God for my own experiences and for my privileged position to write on behalf of so many others. I am profoundly grateful to God for all of you. Thank you, thank you!

> And whatever you do, in word or deed, do everything
> in the name of the Lord Jesus, giving thanks to God the
> Father through him. (Col 3:17, NSRV)

one

INTRODUCTION

"Ring by spring" is the silly notion in Christian universities that the goal of couples (particularly women) is to attain a ring by spring. This puts pressure on people in relationships to commit to one another prematurely, as well as those not involved in relationships, to couple up and rush into a committed relationship.

IT IS FRESHMAN STUDENT orientation weekend at Typical Evangelical Christian University (TECU). Students are busily emptying their cars, saying goodbye to parents and friends, anxiously awaiting the arrival of roommates, and awkwardly engaging in conversation with their new classmates. The new freshmen become aware of the reality of what the next four years entail: challenging courses, choosing a major, exploring new extracurricular activities and groups, learning to fold laundry on their own, trying to manage a healthy diet, and finding time to sleep. Navigating new relationships is somewhat worrisome, but the orientation weekend is packed with opportunities for freshmen to meet other new students and create a social network even before school begins.

While the small, liberal arts Christian university was a comfortable setting for Gina—where faculty, staff, and some students would share her faith convictions and her desire for community—the thought of becoming independent did not come without apprehension. She was used to relying on her close friends and family for emotional support, and secretly dreaded sharing a room with someone other than her sister. She knew she would miss Sunday dinners with her grandparents and the comradery that she had found in her high school youth group. Still, she was thrilled to embark on a new adventure, trusting that TECU would challenge her academically and spiritually. Nonetheless, she enthusiastically arrived on campus, though somewhat fearful of the unknown.

Choosing to go out-of-state for college was not an easy decision for Brent. The idea of independence thrilled him, but the reality did not sit well with him. A star athlete and student in high school, he worried that he would not feel as connected at TECU as he did in high school. He knew that the support and encouragement from his parents motivated him in high school, so he worried about making good decisions about classes, time management, or other extracurricular activities. When his parents had departed earlier that afternoon, his father had declared that he was a now a "man," ready to take on the world. Going to college was hard enough, without the pressure of the idea of becoming an adult overnight.

As Gina, Brent, and five hundred other new students at TECU sat in the university gymnasium together for the first time, a number of administrators, staff, and faculty members warmly welcomed them to campus. Not twenty minutes into the presentation, a faculty member made a quip about "getting that ring by spring!" He chuckled then clarified, "You know. The *engagement* ring! Start saving now, guys!" The next speaker, a representative from Student Life, directed, "Look to your left and to your right, students. You may be sitting next to your future husband or wife. Where else will you find such a large group of eligible, intelligent, Christian men and women?" Finally, nearing the end of this short introductory presentation, a senior student appeared on stage and said with a grin, "They are joking about ring by spring. But just so you know, I did get engaged last spring, and am getting married next summer!"

Gina's heart began to race. She thought to herself, "How exciting! I hope to meet my husband here, too. I long for that intimacy that I am leaving behind. With all of these good Christian men, I'm sure I will find the one God has for me."

Meanwhile, Brent rolled his eyes and joked with the guys around him in the auditorium after the student bragged about getting married. Still, in the back of his mind, he wondered if finding a spouse was something he should consider pursuing. After all, his father had told him he was now a man, and all the good, Christian men he knew were husbands and fathers. Was fin8ding a Christian wife during college something his family expected of him?

The students filed out of the gymnasium and into the cafeteria for their first meal together. Gina found herself checking out her dating options: which of these young men could be her husband? As she scanned the cafeteria to find a place to sit, she began assessing her female peers as well. It was obvious that the competition was fierce: there were at least two young women to every young man. In that moment, Gina began to grow anxious. The pressure seemed to mount as she sat with other young women who were also chatting about the ring by spring comment in the gym. Suddenly, the idea of finding a spouse at college went from an exciting prospect, to anxious concern. What if she graduated without finding her husband? Not only would she continue to feel alone, but she wondered if she could ever find a better dating pool of single Christian men outside of TECU. If she was ever going to find a husband, the next four years would be crucial, she thought.

When Brent and his new friends sat down to eat lunch, they were immediately surrounded by a flock of girls who wanted to know everything about them: where they were from, their majors, whether they had girlfriends. Brent wondered if everyone in the cafeteria was brooding over whether they would also be engaged their senior year. Was this a new dating game he had to learn to play in order to be survive at TECU? How did he know who to date and who not to date? There seemed to be so many options. Brent tensed up and focused on his burger, counting down the minutes to the next activity. He whispered to his friend, "This is going to be a long four years."

In one day, the pressure to find a spouse went from almost nonexistent to socially paralyzing. Both Gina and Brent entered a new phase of life that included more than learning to be an adult, transitioning to college, and committing to a major. This phase appeared to include the added pressure of finding a life partner. In this story, TECU staff and students were playfully commenting on the possibility of finding a life partner in the next four years. For some of those students that possibility may very well become a reality. Many students at Christian colleges and universities do meet their future spouses in college. For others, the failure to meet these cultural expectations could result in an anti-climactic college experience. While they may have achieved academically, socially, or relationally, they fell short of university expectations.

While the characters above are fictional, their stories reflect the experiences of many students at Evangelical Christian universities in the United States today. By incorporating a discussion of marriage into official university programming, the university makes a statement that marriage or engagement is a defining component of student life at the university. Students therefore interpret engagement as an essential component of their university experience, believing it to be a measurement of student success. As a result, one's relationship status could create additional stress for students at a time when they are absorbing every piece of information they can to learn how to succeed in their new college environment.

What Is Ring by Spring?

The term or phrase "ring by spring" (which I will refer to as RxS) signifies Christian college students becoming engaged by spring semester of their senior year. For the most part, engagements are celebratory events, though the concept itself may be pejorative for some. Students use the term to describe couples that appear to be desperate, or mere products of the Christian college environment, with the implication that they are unaware of the profound decision they are making at age twenty-one or twenty-two. Beyond dating and finding a mate, RxS is an underlying cultural current that is heavy-laden with sarcasm, resentment, and assumptions of heteronormativity. This book explores the cultural dynamics found on Christian college campuses that contribute to the unnecessary social pressures for students like Gina and Brent. RxS impacts more than romantic relationships; it influences how students see their peers, their friends, and themselves.

Below are a few examples of student responses when asked to define ring by spring in their own words:

> It means that women and some men that go to college are looking to start courting/dating someone right away in the fall with hopes of getting engaged by the spring.

> Ring by spring is a term used to talk about people that get engaged while in college before spring. It has somewhat become a farce for [our college], almost making fun of the idea of getting married so young in college.

> Social pressure to be engaged before graduating from college; the frequently occurring engagement of couples who date at a Christian college.

> The desperate act of finding a husband before stepping out into the scary real world. I hear it most particularly described as a female goal. I also see it as the idea that finding a husband after school is highly improbable and extremely difficult, which in my opinion is ridiculous.

> The goal of a woman to find a husband by the spring of her final year of college. In my experience, men are not pressured in the same way women are when it comes to this phrase.

> The idea that many Christian college students end up engaged before they graduate, and otherwise something feels off. . . . Mostly a joke, but often true.

These responses are just a fraction of the comments from a research project that began with a campus-wide survey to students at one particular Christian university in 2014. In the survey, I asked students in-depth questions related to their experiences with and their impressions of dating, marriage, and sex. The interest in this topic spread across campus, into the community, even reaching national attention. Literally thousands of Christian college students and alum expressed interest in the project, which turned my original exploratory survey into a three-year data collection process involving content analysis of school newspapers, surveys of students and alumni, and student focus groups. The project intended to explore the various dimensions of dating culture on Christian college campuses and to understand the cultural underpinnings and stigmatization associated with the phrase "ring by spring." The initial findings from 2014 indicated that RxS itself was a reified concept that guided the dating climate on campus. Recognizing the multiple dimensions that embody RxS, my research abruptly turned to an exploration and examination of the implications of RxS on Christian college students today.

Research Overview

The research program I set forth had multiple iterations, which included five phases of research over the course of three years. The *first phase* of research began in 2014 when I conducted an exploratory study with current students at one Christian university. The study included an online anonymous survey with fifty-five closed and open-ended survey questions. I asked students to describe RxS in their own words, share their perspectives on dating, and provide basic demographic information such as gender, age, major, sexuality, and religious affiliation. In a series of open-ended questions, I asked students to explain their perceptions of dating culture on campus, their level of sexual activity, and to describe the settings where they usually talk about issues related to relationships. Given that the RxS culture appears to be perpetuated in Christian places of higher learning, I also asked students to reflect on how the institutional infrastructure may be fostering this culture. The study concluded by seeking information on how, or in what ways, faculty and staff can help facilitate more productive conversations around dating, sex, and marriage. By doing so, perhaps we would be equipped with adequate information on how to address relationship concerns with members of our community, and perhaps we may better serve the young adults in our midst with the necessary tools and procedures to promote healthy relationships.

The *second phase* of research took place in the spring of 2015 when I surveyed students that were engaged or married on one Christian college campus. This study looked primarily at marital preparedness and the resources available to engaged or married couples on campus. I asked questions about premarital counseling or other premarital preparatory activities. I gathered information about materials and mentors that may be resourced prior to engagement or marriage. I also discovered the campus counseling center incorporates a specific curriculum to walk through with discerning couples, engaged couples, or married couples.

The *third phase* of research involved the creation of another survey and incorporated alumni that were recruited to participate through email addresses obtained through the university's alumni office. This resulted in 1,699 responses, 1,675 of which were valid. The sample was convenient, not randomized, but represents a substantial proportion (15 percent) of the overall alumni population available on email. Of the alumni respondents, 35 percent were men, 65 percent were female, and they represented a wide range of graduating cohorts over the last sixty years.

In addition to this survey, I also solicited open-ended comments from alumni at other Evangelical Christian colleges around the country in 2017, which I designate as the *fourth phase* of my research. This was informally distributed via social media and through snowball sampling where one participant would recruit another Christian college alum exposed to RxS culture. Results from phase four are incorporated in this book as anecdotal evidence, or as examples of real situations reported by Christian college alum.

Finally, *the fifth phase* involved focus groups of purposefully selected students who represented various social groups on campus. These focus groups were the final stage in the research process. The intention was to observe students talking about these issues with their peers and to validate or question some of the results from previous findings. These focus groups were recorded with student permission and transcribed excerpts from these conversations are incorporated throughout this book.

The patterns reported here represent a subsection of the larger Christian college population. While the themes presented throughout this book likely reflect experiences of Christian college students around the country, exact statistical measures cannot be generalized to all Christian communities or institutions of Christian higher education. The surveys did not account for regional variation, denominational affiliations of various Christian communities, nor does it control for ranges or levels of religiosity among the participants. However, there are several salient issues that these surveys and focus groups raised that are worthy of consideration and further investigation in our respective communities. My attempt in this book is to highlight these concerns and to suggest theoretical points of departure for more exploratory research on this topic in the future.

Outline

The forthcoming chapters incorporate quotes and stories from various phases of the research. Unless indicated otherwise, each vignette or illustration reported in this book is an actual lived experience of a student or alum, though the names and other identifiable information of those who shared their stories have been anonymized to maintain confidentiality and to protect the privacy of the participants. As a result, this book should be read as a series of narratives, told by Christian college students and alum themselves. I attempt to summarize and interpret the stories as best as possible, but every campus and every student experiences RxS in a unique way. I ask that you join me in reflecting on the intent and the impact of RxS culture by listening deeply to the experiences of the young adults in our midst.

The book proceeds as follows: I begin by explaining the sociocultural dimensions that may have led to the development of

RxS in the twentieth century, and its manifestation today. Chapter 2 looks at the social context and the Christian college students navigating life in the 2010s. I explain some of the developmental issues facing twenty-somethings today and illustrate why marriage at twenty-one or twenty-two may be a greater challenge in the twenty-first century than it was in the past. I also describe the state of marriage in the United States today, as well as the social conditions that may challenge young marriages in the twenty-first century. Finally, I dive into the sociocultural dimensions that make Christian colleges and universities unique places of higher learning, and why these environments are prone to reproduce the RxS ethos.

In chapter 3, I provide a broad description of how RxS has influenced college students on campuses in the contemporary social context. I share information on when the term first developed, according to one Christian college newspaper. I go on to share statistics from the first and third waves of research, which provide some perspective on how students interact with RxS, the social, cultural, religious, and class-based demographics that influence how much pressure students do feel to marry. I conclude by looking at numbers of alumni that actually did marry upon graduation from a Christian college as a gauge to determine just how many students are actually getting their ring by spring. In sum, the number is much lower than most students assume.

In chapter 4, I begin to disaggregate the data and elaborate on how RxS affects men and women in distinct ways. I focus specifically on how women are more likely to feel pressure to marry than men, regardless of sexual orientation. This is due to social pressures outside of the university, as well as internal cultural dynamics (such as gender ratios and peer pressure) that contribute to their stress. I also describe how the four-year time clock of most traditional college students may create added pressure to find a spouse within the short time frame of the college experience.

Chapter 5 expands on gender dynamics and considers how LGBTQ students may experience RxS, or dating in general, on Christian college campuses. Due to the small number of "out"

LGBTQ students on campus, I focus primarily on data collected from focus groups during which students shared their personal stories of being a gay man or lesbian woman on one particular campus, and how ring by spring has or has not impacted the LGBTQ dating culture. This chapter concludes by addressing issues related to sex and the purity culture on Christian campuses. Given the number of books and articles already addressing this issue, my argument, simply stated, is that sexual expression is certainly a cause for young Christians to marry, but it is not the only factor, and sex should be considered as one of many more complex variables.

The conversation then turns to a discussion on the impact of the RxS culture on students. In chapter 6, I explain that while the intention of the culture may not be to harm or to cause anxiety, it is clear that for many students the focus on engagement for all romantic relationships results in confusion, dismissal, and even denial. For students that do not subscribe to the RxS ideology, they are nonetheless influenced by it peripherally, impacting their decisions on who to date, *if* they want to date someone on campus, or even whether they should avoid engagement just to avoid the stereotype of RxS. This includes students that remain single throughout their college years, and how the focus on marriage may lead them to question their sense worth, or whether they belong in the Christian community.

Finally, chapter 7 concludes the book with a discussion on how prepared college students may actually be for marriage. In addition, I provide suggestions on how to better equip students to navigate the path to identity development and positive relationships, while also encouraging them to seek opportunities that exist beyond college. The more we can support our students to choose the path that is best for them—whether that includes dating, marriage, or singleness—the healthier our students will be upon graduation.

two

CHRISTIAN COLLEGES

I didn't think much of it at all at first, kind of an odd joke. But as my years at school continued I began to notice a weird theme: Ring by spring was a thing. Or, at least seemingly half of my friends were in committed relationships, or engaged, and a handful married before school ended or they had a wedding planned. It felt like a weird cultural pressure, not directly but subtly. Just this ever-so-present feeling of mild inadequacy if you didn't at least have "someone." I did have someone and felt a need to get engaged, quickly. I felt like there was an obvious cultural progression that should take place and engagement should be soon. Looking back I kind of laugh at how young I was. I still am with my partner, but we aren't engaged yet—though we are planning on it. We don't feel pressured; at least, I don't really. That insecurity of some kind of timeline is gone, and I'm not sure if that is a subconscious reaction to not being surrounded by a Christian school or if that is my own personal growth.

IN 2013, *THE WASHINGTON Post* published an article titled, "Looking to get married? Try a Christian college." According to the report, a group of Facebook analysts found that 28 percent of people who were married and held a college degree had attended the same college as their spouse. Of the top twenty-five colleges where men are most likely to meet their spouse, all are private Christian institutions. For women, nearly two thirds of the top twenty-five colleges where they are likely to find a husband are religious schools. The twelve schools that appear on both the list for men and women are all Christian colleges. In essence, there is a chance that you could meet your spouse in college, but that chance is even greater if you choose to go to a Christian school.

The results of that study are probably unsurprising for those who either attended Christian colleges, have been employed at one, or have been otherwise affiliated with Christian higher education. Christian colleges tend to attract men and women passionate for learning and passionate about their faith. However, they also attract students that are looking for a strong liberal arts education regardless of its religious affiliation. For those students coming from families with traditional family structures and conservative Christian values, the college years may be the time they anticipate finding a husband or wife. Those students do not hesitate or shy away from pursuing serious relationships, generating the striking statistics cited in the *Post* article above. Knowing how many students come to college with this mindset remains a mystery (and is an excellent future research project for an ambitious scholar). Still, the perpetuation of ring by spring—that is, a culture that encourages, if not expects, students to meet their future spouse during the four of five years of their undergraduate career—is also a product of Christian colleges themselves.

In order to fully understand the dynamics of RxS, strict dating patterns, and the pressure to marry (and marry young), it is imperative to recognize the context in which this phenomenon takes place, and the student population Christian colleges serve. The intersection of age, religion, and other demographic qualities make Christian colleges particularly fertile grounds for finding a mate.

College Students Today

In the last two decades, psychologists and sociologists have identified a new developmental stage: post-adolescence and pre-adulthood. In the United States, adulthood has historically been understood to include the following developmental milestones: moving out of one's parent's home, becoming financially independent, completing (or mostly completing) education, choosing a career, marrying, and having children. In the current social context, most traditional college graduates (approximately twenty-two to twenty-four year olds) have only completed one—if any—of these developmental tasks. Nonetheless, the decisions that they make during their college years set the stage for their true adulthood, including major selection, career selection, city of residence, and relationship status. Thus, in the twenty-first century, individuals aged eighteen to twenty-four are now considered to represent a transition from late adolescence to the early adulthood developmental stage known as "emerging adulthood." During this phase of life, emerging adults experiment with a variety of social roles that may lead to the possibility of future identities (possible career paths, social interests, group identification). According to the *New York Times*:

> It's happening all over, in all sorts of families, not just young people moving back home but also young people taking longer to reach adulthood overall. It's a development that predates the current economic doldrums, and no one knows yet what the impact will be—on the prospects of the young men and women; on the parents on whom so many of them depend; on society, built on the expectation of an orderly progression in which kids finish school, grow up, start careers, make a family and eventually retire to live on pensions supported by the next crop of kids who finish school, grow up, start careers, make a family and on and on. The traditional cycle seems to have gone off course, as young people remain untethered to romantic partners or to permanent homes, going back to school for lack of better options, traveling, avoiding commitments, competing ferociously

for unpaid internships or temporary (and often grueling) Teach for America jobs, forestalling the beginning of adult life.[1]

This new reality leads us to question the structure of higher education itself, and the demand it places on students who have just begun to define their personal and social identities. For example, when students enter college, they are typically expected to declare a major within the first two years. Yet, according to the National Center for Education Statistics, about 50 percent of students enter college undecided about their major, and 80 percent of students in the United States end up changing their major at least once[2] due to role experimentation and identity development apart from the identity and expectations imposed upon them in their families of origin. Choosing a career is a lifelong decision, but unlike marriage, for example, career decisions are more easily reversible or exchangeable.

One of the most pressing concerns is whether college students today are capable of recognizing the significance of marriage, or whether they are blinded by the immediate goal of RxS without understanding the full extent of its implications. Beyond finding someone that is like-minded, Christian colleges also tend to promote traditional marriage values, which may or may not resonate with all students on campus, especially as society becomes more progressive. Understanding the sociological processes involved in mate selection, in addition to gauging marriage trends in the United States, will provide a deeper appreciation of the sociocultural context that breeds RxS culture.

1. Henig, "What," para. 2.
2. NCES, "Data Point."

Mate Selection and
Marriage Trends in the United States

For traditional undergraduate students,[3] going to college[4] has both intended and unintended outcomes. The obvious outcome of college attendance is a degree, with the prospect of gainful employment and a profitable career. Beyond being just factories of knowledge, colleges provide job training through internships and externships, and provide opportunities for professional networking. Studies show that health, happiness, political attitudes, civic participation, cultural preferences, and social capital expansion results from a college experience.

College attendance also has unintended outcomes as well, such as meeting friends, expanding one's social and cultural capital, and meeting a future spouse. In college, people tend to gather with others that share common social characteristics such as age, educational level, and cultural values. One study found that college graduates are increasingly likely to marry each other. This "educational assortative mating"[5] argues that people marry people like themselves since those with similar education and earnings potential will likely reflect similar values and lifestyle choices.[6] In fact, according to one study, people are now more likely to marry others with similar educational attainment—even after controlling for differences between men and women, like the fact that women were once less likely to attend college.[7] Moreover, college graduates

3. Traditional undergraduate students are typically considered to be those who enroll in college immediately after high school and pursue college studies full-time. Traditional students typically complete a bachelor's degree program in four or five years at the age of twenty-two or twenty-three, are financially dependent on others, usually do not have children, and are employed only on a part-time basis.

4. Traditional, brick-and-mortar, four-year degree granting institution. May be public or private.

5. Mare, "Five," 15.

6. Miller and Bui, "Equality."

7. Mare, "Five."

often marry other college graduates who attended schools of the same type (for example, elite male or female only universities).[8]

Another study reported that the highest rate of marriage occurred at private religious schools, with 43 percent of students married by the time they reach age twenty-three to twenty-five.[9] This is in comparison to other selective liberal arts colleges with marriage rates as low as 0.9 percent to 1.5. Selective liberal arts schools are more likely to send large percentages of their students to graduate school—a factor which tends to delay marriage. The study also found that students in an older cohort (those born in the early 1980s, as opposed to those born in the early 1990s) held significantly higher marriage rates, whereas those colleges with the highest rates in student marriage had rates over 80 percent among students in their early thirties. For non-Christian liberal arts schools, the older cohort had marriage rates close to 60 percent. In essence, most students are unlikely to get married if attending a non-Christian affiliated college, though more likely to get married young if attending a Christian college.

The implications of this finding are not trivial. Choosing to marry over going to graduate school, for example, has been linked with substantial social and economic consequences for individuals, particularly for women. Information from the National Campaign to Prevent Teen and Unplanned Pregnancy, the National Marriage Project at the University of Virginia, and the RELATE Institute, reveal that delaying marriage allows both men and women to pursue post-graduate education, establish themselves in their career, and become financially stable. The economic benefits of waiting to get married more greatly impacts women, as it implies that women are investing in their future career and earning potential. According to one study, women may make as much as $18,000 more per year if they wait until their thirties to marry.[10] Conversely, there are ramifications for delaying marriage as well. Other research from the National Marriage Project tells us that unmarried individuals

8. Arum, Roksa, and Budig, "Romance," 107.

9. Kelchen, "Examining," para. 6.

10. Hymowitz et al., "Knot Yet."

in their twenties are more likely to be depressed, and report lower levels of life satisfaction than their married peers.

But is marriage really an appropriate solution to decreasing one's risk of depression or assurance of overall "life satisfaction"? Putting these expectations on marriage could harm future marriages by preemptively placing so many personal beliefs on the marriage. This way of interpreting marriage is relatively new. Up until the end of the eighteenth century, emotional expectations and romantic feelings of love had almost nothing to do with marriage. Marriage used to be an economic incentive and social status symbol, if not a requirement for adults in the United States.

In 1960 the average age of marriage was twenty-two for men and twenty-three for women. By the early twentieth century, however, perspectives on marriage changed, as romantic ideations associated with love became the US cultural norm for marrying. By 2010, the average age of marriage was twenty-eight for men, and twenty-six for women, a significant change in just a half century. Now, national studies indicate that most millennials will marry about five years later (on average) than their parents.[11] About 50 percent of Americans marry by age thirty, 75 percent by the age of thirty-five, and 85 percent by the age of forty.[12]

11. According to the Pew Research Center, a millennial is anyone born between 1981 and 1996.

12. Vital and Health Statistics report from the CDC: "Cohabitation."

Figure 2.1 Average Age of Marriage in the US (1960–2010)[13]

Stephanie Coontz, author of *Marriage, a History: How Love Conquered Marriage*, writes:

> The historical transformation in marriage over the ages has created a similar paradox for society as a whole. Marriage has become more joyful, more loving, and more satisfying for many couples than ever before in history. At the same time it has become optional and more brittle. These two strands of change cannot be disentangled.[14]

Traditional expectations for marriage have been preserved, but without the same purpose. Rather than marrying for economic security, marriage has become an institution valued by society for the maintenance of traditional social norms, led largely by traditional forces in the church. Conservative evangelical church subcultures emphasize traditional family ideologies and have established mega-organizations that oversee the preservation of these values, such as the Focus on the Family Institute. While there is nothing inherently wrong with choosing to have a traditional marriage and family structure, the trouble arises when others who do not share those values, even within the Christian community, are supposed to uphold and fulfill the expectations of the traditionalists.

13. US Census Bureau, "Figure MS-2."
14. Coontz, *Marriage*, 306.

Nearly every study conducted on religious, social, and political demographics in the United States has indicated that younger generations are more progressive than older generations, which challenges the traditional structures protected by those in conservative Christian subcultures. One way this is manifested is in how evangelicals approach name changes in heterosexual marriages. One research project worked with students at four evangelical universities around the issue regarding marriage and marital name changes. Of the 199 students surveyed, only one student did not plan to marry (0.5 percent of the population). They write, "Marriage is an anticipated rite of passage for these students. Choosing to attend an Evangelical college may be an intentional step toward this rite. Finding a spouse may not be in the promotional materials, but it is a selling point for these colleges."[15]

The studies above suggest that it is possible to meet your spouse at college, though rarely, if ever, would a public school promote marriage as a reason to enroll. If finding a spouse is a selling point for Christian colleges and universities, there are internal cultural dynamics that make them particularly opportunistic environments. Why is this?

Are engagements and marriage rates higher at Christian colleges because university officials coordinate more opportunities to date?

Are rates higher because there are long-standing traditions of engagement and marriage that have yet to be challenged?

Are Christian colleges prolific places to find a spouse because there are more students enrolling in Christian colleges looking for a spouse?

Or is it the combination of religion, age, interest, and other homogenous features that make it more possible for students to find their match?

The answer to all of the above is yes. Here is why:

15. Dougherty, Hulbert, and Palmer, "Marital," 1126.

The Christian College Setting

The term "Christian colleges" refers to the 150 schools in the United States and Canada affiliated with the Council for Christian Colleges and Universities (CCCU). According to the organization:

> CCCU institutions are accredited, comprehensive colleges and universities whose missions are Christ-centered and rooted in the historic Christian faith. Most also have curricula rooted in the arts and sciences. The CCCU's mission is to advance the cause of Christ-centered higher education and to help our institutions transform lives by faithfully relating scholarship and service to biblical truth.[16]

CCCU affiliated schools pride themselves in being distinctly [Protestant] Christian, and decisively different from other private and public universities. As society became more and more progressive in the 1960s and '70s, Christian colleges represented, and continue to represent, a cultural outlet that preserved traditional structures that would protect young adults from exposure to the outside world until they were properly equipped with a Christian education to tackle the life challenges that awaited them. Rather than just a place of higher learning that awards degrees after four or five years, CCCU institutions make college a complete experience: educational, spiritual, and relational. Spirituality and faith integration is fundamental to the educational experience. All faculty and staff members are expected—if not required—to be active members of a Christian community or church. As a result, students are ministered to by their faculty and staff mentors. Regardless of whether students are Christian themselves, they receive the same Christ-centered curricular structure that is valued and pursued in these settings.

Christian colleges and universities have student-centered activities like other traditional colleges and universities, including student body governance, athletics, theater, etc. In addition to the standard clubs, Christian schools also offer regular chapel and

16. CCCU, "Advancing," para. 1.

worship services, Bible studies, and other small group opportunities for spiritual growth. According to the CCCU, "Our purpose is to form students of moral commitment who live out Christian virtues such as love, courage, and humility. This task gives meaning and coherence to every part of the academy, from the classroom to the fine arts studio, from the internship placement to the residence hall and the athletic field."[17]

Most Christian colleges are small, meaning the traditional undergraduate population is typically less than 5,000, though the average is more likely to be around 1,500. As a result, fostering community and building intentional relationships tend to be core themes across Christian college campuses. There are plenty of school-sponsored activities that expand beyond the standard practices mentioned above. Instead, residence directors, student life staff, and student leaders will organize social activities that can happen on or off campus to encourage deeper relationships with one another. For example, some Christian colleges establish brother or sister dorms or floors. They plan group activities, have Bible studies together, pray for each other, eat together, and may even have special visitation rights; Christian colleges often have restricted visitation hours in dorms, or require doors to be open when members of the other gender are inside. It is the Christian version of Greek campus life, without alcohol, aggressive hazing, or sex.

Thus, the intensity and focus on forming relationships is a pervasive theme across Christian college campuses. This includes both romantic and non-romantic relationships. Same-gender platonic relationships are invested in within residence halls and student life activities. Not surprisingly, then, non-platonic relationships are also formed across (and sometimes within) gender groups. CCCU schools incorporate traditions that are remarkably heteronormative, and built on the anticipation of romantic relationship formation.

Relationships on Christian campuses have been described as a "clash between espoused beliefs, policies, and day-to-day

17. CCCU, "Advancing," para 9.

practice."[18] As Dana Malone, author of *From Single to Serious*, describes it:

> Going to dinner and a movie is no longer a means to get to know someone with whom you have little familiarity. Rather, dating for these students is a significant commitment; it is only a few short steps away from the altar.[19]

Though the theological, regional, academic, and cultural diversity across Christian colleges is limited in to "large" and "small" in Malone's book, the author describes student experiences of dating culture at Christian colleges similarly to the ways students in the ring by spring study describe it.

As the years pass, societies generally become more progressive, challenging or erasing traditional, often conservative, cultural values. Yet, traditionalism remains a cornerstone feature of Christian living in most contexts, representing a clear counter-cultural dynamic that makes Christian environments (e.g., colleges) unique from other public and private spaces. Marriage and engagement at Christian colleges is not only normal, but it actually goes directly against dating culture at most public and non-religiously affiliated liberal arts colleges, which tend to perpetuate "hook-up" culture, "brief, uncommitted sexual encounters between individuals who are not romantic partners or dating each other,"[20] where sexual relationships are dismissive, or casual at best.

This is in complete opposition to the "sexual purity to life-long commitment" culture of dating found at many Christian colleges in the United States, representing a cultural shift in openness and acceptance of uncommitted sexual relationships. What is more, some schools actually provide opportunities to date a member of the opposite gender in campus-sponsored activities or traditions. For example, residence life staff arrange a date night for the same-gender dorm floor in an activity called "Roomies" or "Get Your Roommate a Date." Here, the roommates choose dates

18. Malone, *From Single to Serious*, 29.

19. Malone, *From Single to Serious*, 18.

20. Garcia et al., "Sexual," 161.

for the other, resulting in a number of blind dates on the night of the event. The resident assistant then coordinates the activity (e.g., a trip to the zoo, bowling, pizza and a sporting event, etc.). Some colleges even coordinate matchmaking activities during freshman orientation. For example, each student must "propose marriage" to three strangers they want to get to know better; or, playing a game where freshmen men have to make freshmen women smile while she sits on his knee.

In a blog called "The Pietist Schoolman," historian and Christian college professor Chris Gehrz writes, "It's clear that many prospective students and their parents are considering [Christian colleges] precisely because they're thinking ahead to marriage, and I'm not sure we do much to discourage such intentions."[21] It seems evident that some Christian colleges are more forthcoming with the RxS issue than others. For example, some Christian schools have admitted that telling students they can find their mate is used as a "recruiting tool"[22] to attract prospective students. Some colleges have school traditions during orientation weekend that require freshmen to participate in heteronormative matchmaking games with brother or sister dorms. Other schools have a ceremonial bell on campus that engaged couples are meant to ring together after their engagement happens. Still other schools are making a concerted effort to remove any such culture from formal campus practices. One school actually removed the "ring by spring" phrase from student life materials as a symbolic representation of the university moving away from the culture.

Most Christian colleges do encourage their prospective and current students to ponder big life questions around careers and family during college. While not all Christian colleges reinforce the expectation that students should be marriage-minded throughout college, data reveal that students nonetheless experience this pressure from their peers, parents, churches, and other social influences, if not in their schools. One institution has proactively attempted to distract students from RxS, with the intention

21. Gehrz, "Marriage," para. 5.
22. Adams, "Ring," para. 5.

of encouraging and fostering positive and healthy relationships across all genders. However, that has not led to the disappearance of marital pressures and expectations. The culture of RxS runs deep, having established a cultural history embedded in student concerns since the early years of Christian higher education.

Conclusion

For some students, attendance at Christian colleges may be due to the intention of finding a future spouse. If these notions are not found in promotional materials at these schools then how is the culture perpetuated? What is its impact on the student population at Christian colleges, and what can Christian leaders at these institutions do to address issues related to marriage and dating on college campuses properly? Because whether or not RxS is perpetuated by institutional leaders, it is nonetheless a reality that surrounds us and is more than worthy of our attention and concern. Some may mock the absurdity of dating culture on Christian campuses, believing the impact on student life to be miniscule in the short term, the reality is that the consequences of these strict dating rituals results in feelings of failure and worthlessness in the long run for those who graduate without a partner.

three

SETTING THE SCENE

> I get this notion that because [our campus community] is so small that as soon as you go on a date with someone everyone is talking about you. That, in turn, results in this weird pressure to feel committed to someone that you just went on a date with. Like one date. And that has, consequently, resulted in the lack of a dating culture. A casual dating culture.

I RECENTLY ATTENDED A wedding between two former Christian college students. It was a perfect wedding: the kind where everyone knew the couple was perfect for each other. The ceremony was a true celebration of their love and commitment to one another, and to their relationship in Christ. During the service, the pastor who was officiating the ceremony told the story of how the couple had met during their first semester in college. He joked, "Even though they have technically graduated, she still managed to get that ring by spring!" The couple and the guests chuckled, and a few people, including a member of the wedding party, glanced in my direction. I smirked at the irony of the phrase in this context. True, this couple met in college, and married shortly after graduation. By definition, they exemplified the quintessential RxS experience. Nevertheless, the phrase "ring by spring" is singed with so much cynicism it seems sacrilegious to even mention it at a wedding. Even though they had met in college, became engaged during their final year, and married shortly thereafter, they were truly meant for each other; they were not one of *those* (stereotypical RxS) couples who were rushing to marry, despite their lack of preparation. This particular couple was considered the exception. These two were not like the others, so it was considered socially acceptable to joke about it.

Or is it?

Why laugh? Is RxS a joke? Why do people immersed in the culture brush it off as an inconsequential product of Christian dating culture? It should be clear by now that RxS in and of itself is not just about student engagement or marriage. RxS is a cultural paradox; it is both encouraged and discouraged by the campus community. It celebrates engagements while also chiding those who fit the stereotype. It is about the pressure to fit in to a culture that persists because of social interactions among Christian college students. Yet, regardless if a student is involved in a stereotypical Christian college relationship, or observing from the outside, almost all students are keenly aware of its existence. One student described this situation in the following way:

> I feel like there is this cloud over Christian colleges. It's not like the college president is saying, "Get your ring by spring!" It's not one person. It's a culture. It's like this cloud just envelops everyone. So all of our conversations—even if you are single—end in, "Oh, so are you getting married soon?" We all fall into these conversational patterns ourselves.

The phrase "ring by spring" may be foreign to some, though the concept is familiar to many. The notion that a student becomes engaged by the time he or she graduates in order to fulfill cultural expectations is especially pronounced in Christian young adult circles. "Ring by spring or your [tuition] money back!" some may say. It carries with it a demeaning tone, even though the outcome— engagement—is widely celebrated. For those outside of Christian circles, this may seem like an antiquated, or even ironic, cultural practice. Even for some *inside* Christian circles, RxS seems like a cultural product of the past, though in reality, the term is relatively new, even if the idea is antiquated.

According to a survey of Christian college alumni, 95 percent who have graduated within the past twenty years (class of 1996 onward) have at least heard of RxS, whereas only 56 percent of alumni from 1986 to 1995, and 52 percent of alumni from 1976 to 1985, have heard of RxS. Only 42 percent of those that graduated prior to 1975 have heard of the term, though that does not necessarily mean they were unfamiliar with the concept. According to a content analysis[1] of a Christian college school newspaper, the phrase "ring by spring" did not enter the college lexicon as a concept until the 1990s, when the idea of marrying someone in college became an anecdote or a poke at students representing an outdated perspective on marriage. Table 3.1 below shows how marriage was depicted in the newspaper over the course of several decades.

Finding a spouse in college developed in an era where marrying at age twenty-one was the cultural norm. The traditional family structure encouraged by Christian colleges remained as society progressed, marriage rates dropped, and the average age of first marriage increased. It was about this time that young marriages became counter-cultural to the rest of society. Christian colleges maintained a traditional perspective on dating and sex, and thereby represented a culture different from the mainstream. However, as the traditional lens on dating and marriage began to clash with social norms outside of Christian colleges, the term was introduced and became a popular tagline for student relationships that epitomized Christian college culture itself. Given the close cultural connection across Christian institutions, it is probable that most Christian colleges have a similar written—or unwritten—student cultural code that anticipates engagement and marriage across the student population.

1. A content analysis is a research method that involves coding for themes apparent in preexisting data. In this case, school newspapers.

	1909–1929	1930–1949	1950–1969	1969–1989	1990–2005	2006–2010	Total
Table 3.1 Christian College Newspaper Depictions of Ring by Spring							
Marriage as Christian college tradition	0	1	0	0	11	13	25
Marriage announcement	0	18	5	0	0	0	23
Engagement announcement	2	5	11	0	0	0	18
RxS as cultural tradition	0	0	0	0	5	13	18
Marriage as pressure	0	0	0	2	1	7	10
Marriage as gender expectation	0	0	0	3	2	5	10
RxS as harmful	0	0	0	0	2	6	8
Marriage as girl's desire	0	1	0	0	1	3	7
Marriage as sacrifice	0	0	0	3	3	0	6
Marriage as God's will	0	0	0	0	2	4	6
Marriage as rational next step	0	0	0	1	2	3	6
Marriage as fear of divorce	0	0	0	0	2	2	4
Marriage as an expectation	0	0	0	0	1	3	4
Marriage advertisement	0	2	0	2	0	0	4
Marriage as symbol	0	0	0	1	0	2	3
RxS as serious	0	0	0	0	2	1	3
RxS as legacy	0	0	0	0	2	1	3
Warning of divorce	0	0	0	0	0	3	3
Generational marriage trends	0	0	0	0	1	1	2
Marriage caution (for women)	0	0	0	0	1	1	2

The Pressure to Marry

College students across the United States, regardless of university affiliations, are reporting high rates of anxiety to succeed in college academically and professionally. According to the 2017 National College Health Assessment survey, 60 percent of men and 78 percent of women report feeling overwhelmed in the last month, and 91 percent report experiencing average to tremendous amount of stress in the last year. The mounting pressure emerging adults feel to succeed or fit in is higher than at any point in documented history. Be it related to identity issues (race, gender, sexual orientation), or increased financial strain, or even peer expectation as prompted by social media outlets, social pressures are not uncommon to this population.

Additional sources of anxiety and stress may exist at Christian universities. This includes the weight of finding a serious relationship. In a survey of alumni at one particular Christian college, alumni were asked whether they recalled feeling pressure to marry when in college, and if so, from where the pressure came (see Figure 3.1 below).

Figure 3.1 Pressure to marry during college

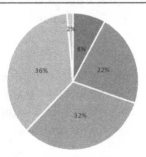

Definitely – 8%   A little bit – 22%   Not really – 32%   Not at all – 36%   Already married – 2%

It is extremely important to note that of all alumni respondents to this question (a total of 1,639 respondents), more than half claim to not have felt any pressure. However, if we break down the source of pressure further, by grouping responses by graduating cohort, we begin to see that more recent cohorts report pressure more than older graduating cohorts (see Table 3.2 below).

Table 3.2 Source of Pressure by Graduating Cohort

Graduat-ing Year	No pressure	Parents	Peers	Religious Institu-tions	Sig-nificant Other	Society	College faculty/ staff	Total (n)
2012–2017	12.6%	8.7%	28.4%	15.4%	6.8%	23.5%	4.69%	469
2007–2011	11.5%	14.4%	35.2%	0.0%	7.8%	27.0%	4.07%	270
1996–2006	18.6%	6.8%	30.0%	14.3%	5.6%	21.0%	3.86%	414
1986–1995	26.0%	10.2%	18.1%	11.0%	6.3%	26.8%	1.57%	127
1976–1985	27.8%	12.2%	12.2%	15.6%	11.1%	18.9%	2.22%	90
Before 1975	53.6%	4.3%	22.5%	0.0%	18.1%	0.0%	1.45%	138

Students that graduated after 1996 were more likely to report some pressure than the earlier cohorts. Note that 53 percent of the graduating class prior to 1975 do *not* report feeling pressure. This is a striking finding; in this particular school context, as society progresses and the average marriage rates of individuals in the United States are extending into their late twenties, the pressure to marry while in college is actually *increasing*. Although the pressure to marry may only impact half of the student population, this finding nonetheless warrants further discussion into the current situation facing Christian college students.

Dating and the Road to Engagement

RxS implies marriage, but neglects the process to get there almost entirely. Often the *process* necessary to find a spouse is overlooked in the hurriedness to find a spouse. What does this dating culture look like on college campuses? One student attempted to explain the difference between "normal" dating (his words) and RxS dating in the following way:

> I am dating with the intent to marry someday, hopefully. But that's different from, "I am dating you because I want to marry." That is what makes ring by spring different. I don't know exactly where that line is, but [in a Christian College environment] it's pretty blurry.

This is certainly true at Christian colleges, but it can also be seen in Christian dating cultures outside of higher education. This list of "don'ts" (don't date, don't lust, don't be "impure," don't be a tease) that the Christian church readily shares is more accessible than the list of "dos." As a result, single adults may find dating especially confusing or even intimidating. Some Christian "how to date" guides have provided a seemingly unrealistic standard for the single Christian. The evangelical purity movement is a prominent cultural standard in conservative Christian cultures. The idea is that men and women should not date at all, but rather engage in "courtship" as a way to find a spouse. The message is that dating connects a person to other people, and that each time an individual finds a new boyfriend of girlfriend, they are giving away a piece of their heart that should be kept in tact for their future spouse. The problem with this process is that it becomes unclear on how to meet or get to know anyone at all if dating wasn't an option. Below is an example of this expectation, taken from Joshua Harris's iconic non-dating book, *I Kissed Dating Goodbye*.[2]

> In recent years, I've tried to let God's love as displayed at the cross define the way I love members of the opposite sex. This kind of love leads to some very practical changes in the way a person approaches relationships. Personally, I've come to some pretty intense conclusions for my life. I've come to realize that while friendships with the opposite sex are great, I have no business asking for a girl's heart and exclusive affections if I'm not ready to consider

---

2. The book's author, Joshua Harris, has since made a film about surviving this practically impossible and theologically flawed advice.

marriage. Until I can do that, I'd only be using that girl to meet my short term needs, not seeking to bless her for the long term. Would I enjoy having a girlfriend right now? You bet! But I wouldn't truly be loving her and putting her interests first.[3]

Honoring every man and woman is a virtuous endeavor and certainly respect should be forefront when dating or courting. Yet again, the practicality of assuming a person knows another well enough to consider marriage before dating turns out to be more complicated. Perhaps the reason students pursue marriage at such a young age is they misinterpret the purpose of dating; or perhaps they believe that dating a person who may or not may not be their future spouse as relationally irresponsible.

More recently, Christian authors have countered the courtship model and have encouraged Christian men and women instead to kiss dating hello. Debra Fileta published a book called, *True Love Dates* (a play on the purity movement's phrase "true love waits"), which encourages young men and women to feel comfortable with themselves and comfortable with God before pursuing relationships. She encourages single men and women to wait to pursue marriage until the timing is right; that is, when a person has clearly identified their significant other as an emotionally secure and spiritually healthy partner. She warns against going too deep too fast, arguing that emotional intimacy can take a person further into a relationship than perhaps it should go early on.[4]

Fileta's message seems to bridge Christianity with contemporary dating cultural norms. Still, the relationship guidelines outlined by the purity movement informed the primary message preached in many evangelical youth group cultures for decades. Thus, the courtship model transferred onto Christian colleges as the norm for student dating. But not all students buy into that model.

According to the survey of current students, nearly one-third of students believe dating is a process where you meet other people,

3. Harris, *Kissed*, 19.
4. Fileta, *True Love Dates*.

not necessarily with the intention to marry. Another quarter or so believe dating is a social process that is necessary to find a spouse, while the last quarter believe you should only date seriously, with the intention to marry.

Table 3.3 Perspectives on Dating	
Meet other people, not necessarily with the intention to marry	33.5%
A social process necessary to find a spouse	27.7%
Only date seriously, with the intention to marry	23.7%
Get to know as many people as you can	4.6%
Other	2.3%
No interest in dating	1.7%
No Answer	6.4%

While one person may believe that dating is a social process, another person may believe that dating should only occur when seeking a spouse. Given the range of perspectives of dating on campus, couples may find themselves in precarious situations where one is expecting an engagement ring by the end of the first month, while another may see the relationships as much more casual. This leads to the Christian college dating verbiage of "DTR" (defining the relationship) so that both people understand the implications of their relationship. This can undoubtedly make the situation more complicated, and more serious in nature, even if the intentions of one person are relatively benign or experimental. Thus, some students choose not to date at all! One student explained this dynamic in the following statement:

> In my perspective, [the Christian college] breeds an environment where men are afraid to ask out a girl because there is pressure to marry that person right away. While I do believe we should date intentionally, I do not believe that we know on a first date if we will marry them.

While there is nothing wrong with being interested in marriage, RxS culture may perpetuate a sense of desperation to achieve this goal.

The Source(s) of Pressure

From where does this pressure to marry come? Who or what is to blame for the perpetuation of a dating environment that could be harmful to young people? The answer may not be as straight-forward as one might think. Despite the fact that RxS is part of the Christian college lexicon, and is a dynamic pervasive on their campuses, the schools themselves are seldom to blame. In the initial exploratory survey, students reported that professors and student life staff on campuses were among the lowest groups contributing to the pressures associated with RxS. Instead, students reported that peer groups (33 percent), family (26 percent), churches (24 percent), and society at-large (34 percent) were the greatest sources of pressure to marry.

It is therefore reasonable to conclude that students are also socialized by marriage values while in college. How each student experienced those values will vary dramatically, but one alum equated her observations to "an overly simplistic version of 'let's play house.'" However, her socialization from outside the RxS "norm" led her to critically question the value of marrying while in college, even encouraging university staff to question the culture itself, instead of relying on students to establish norms for dating and engagement. She writes:

> Having witnessed my parents' marriage, and those of many adult friends both before and after my time at Whitworth, I feel that my understanding of marriage is (I hope) more nuanced than what I witnessed and was "taught" in college.

Parents undoubtedly shape the marriage expectations of their children. In the reported data from students, parents clearly contributed to their children's behaviors and values of marriage. They also affected how students approached mate selection while they were in college, for better or for worse. For some students, parental divorce was a factor that kept them from pursuing relationships. For others, the marriage relationship they witnessed between their parents was something they wanted to experience themselves.

In a similar finding, students who prayed often, indicating a commitment to their Christian faith, were more likely to experience a great amount of pressure. Other factors, such as parent's marital status and parent's religion, were not significant findings, statistically. The influence of religion on one's perception of whether they should be married is a pervasive theme throughout the quantitative and qualitative results of the study. I elaborate on the nuances of these findings in the next few chapters.

Socialization does not begin and end with parenting or family values. Church attendance is another factor that contributes to values associated with marriage. The varying levels of religiosity among students at Christian colleges should also be taken into consideration. Again, students reported that peer groups, family, churches, and society in general were among the highest social groups that encouraged marriage. For those students that attended church regularly, their sense of pressure was significantly higher than those who attended church less frequently.

Table 3.4 Pressure to Marry and Church Attendance

		Do you feel pressured to be married?					
		Definitely	A little bit	Not really	Not at all	Already married	Total
How often do you attend church?	Never	0	4	2	9	1	16
	Once or twice a year	0	7	2	3	1	13
	A few times a year	1	8	5	4	0	18
	Once a month	2	9	6	6	1	24
	Once a week	12	23	13	2	2	52
	At least once a week	6	15	6	5	1	33
	Total	21	66	34	29	6	156

From this cross tabulation, we can assume that churches may be contributing to pressures to marry. Unfortunately, this study does not address the internal dynamics of churches that may prove or disprove this hypothesis. However, later I revisit the impact of religiosity on student's pressure to marry in light of traditional Christian perspectives related to sex and gender.

Is Everyone Engaged or Married?

Students operate under the assumption that marriage or engagement before graduation is the norm among their peers. When asked if students wanted to marry someday, 86 percent responded affirmatively (12 percent were unsure, 2 percent did not want to marry). Surprisingly, however, students do not *expect* to be married in college, despite the culture. The Christian university where the study was conducted does not have accurate statistics on how many students do actually become engaged during their college years, student's perceptions of how many students actually *do* become engaged is vastly exaggerated. I asked students whether they anticipated becoming engaged or being married when they graduated. Only 6.3 percent of students said that they were, in fact, engaged or were planning to become engaged before graduation. Given the pressure felt by most students in the survey, there is an evident disconnect between expectations, perception, and reality.

The best RxS statistics to date come from self-reporting in the alumni survey. While it is difficult to evaluate its reliability or generalizability, it is worth mentioning that in one Christian college, most alumni married between ages twenty-two and twenty-five, though only 371 (21.9 percent) of alumni respondents were engaged or married when they graduated (only 13.01 were engaged, 9.5 were married). Of those that were married or engaged, 274 (74 percent) remained married or engaged, 77 (20.7 percent) divorced or separated, 13 (3.5 percent) were widowed, and 7 (1.8 percent) never married. This is over the course of forty-five-plus years. Looking just at graduates from 1996 onward, once, according to the student newspaper, "ring by spring" became a catchphrase on campus and students began reporting the phrase as a source of pressure, only 11 percent graduated engaged and 4 percent graduated as a married person.

Clearly the perception that "everyone gets engaged during college" is flawed, and if the CCCU institutions wanted to make engagement and marriage a measurable goal then they have a long way to go. However, I do not think most institutions really expect this of students, rather they see strong Christian romantic relationships as a by-product of student attendance and retention. Indeed, a number of students may be engaged by the time the graduate, but the reality is that few actually do get married in this time frame.

Regardless of whether institutions specifically target single students, the impact of the presence of RxS has left a lasting impression on those who failed to exchange engagement rings prior to graduation. In response to the question, "How did it feel to be single when you graduated?" One alum answered, "I felt a bit vulnerable, disappointed, and like I had done something wrong. I felt even embarrassed." Though marriage can be a progressive milestone for many graduates, it is not the only milestone. Students should not feel like they have failed if they are not engaged to be married when they receive their degree.

Table 3.5 Relationship Status upon Graduation	
Single	48.5%
Casually dating	6.8%
In a committed relationship	21.7%
Engaged	13.0%
Married	9.5%
Divorced	0.4%

Who Is Married?

So who is the "stereotypical couple"? Who is most likely to end up with an engagement ring? According to students, it was anyone who was at a Christian college that became engaged during college. I expand this question to include specific demographic information. Men and women are equally as likely to be engaged, with two thirds remaining single upon graduation, and one third engaged or married (see Table 3.6). This should not be surprising, since theoretically, most men are giving engagement rings to women. Exceptions are when partners are either not in school, already graduated, or on another campus. In each of these cases, these couples would not fit the traditional RxS model since they did not meet, date, and marry at a Christian college.

Table 3.6 Marital Status upon Graduation by Gender

	Single	Engaged or Married
Men	377 (66%)	194 (34%)
Women	711 (65.3%)	377 (34.6%)

Religion, race, and the intersection between the two were significantly impactful variables to determine whether a student was engaged or married upon graduation. A student's religious tradition was a stronger predictor of RxS status upon graduation in comparison to race. White Protestant Christians and non-white Protestant Christians had higher rates of engagements and marriages than non-Protestants. Thus, a student who is non-white and non-Protestant is not only a cultural minority on college campuses with respect to religion or race, but they are less likely to fit the cultural norm of securing an engagement ring.

This finding does not mean that students who do not meet the "white Protestant" mold are immune from the pressure of RxS. One current student explained,

> I recently got into a relationship. I identify as Christian, and so does my partner. But I do not fit the typical Christian college stereotype: both of us are people of color, not wealthy, I'm pretty liberal. But we even unknowingly started to talk about marriage not even realizing that we were falling into the weird ring by spring culture.

Conversations about racial disparity on Christian college campuses are worthy of an entire book in and of itself. Indeed, many colleges in the Council for Christian Colleges and Universities consortium struggle with attracting a student population from diverse backgrounds. Thus, the racial and cultural majority on Christian college campuses is white Protestantism, which suggests that RxS is also a product of this majority culture.

Positive Responses

Responses to the surveys were overwhelmingly focused on the negative consequences of their exposure to the RxS culture. The repetition of words like "pressure" and "fear" and sentiments of individual failure and unworthiness occupied most of the open-ended responses. Surely, there were individuals with positive experiences. Where were the students and alumni who married their college sweetheart and lived happily ever after?

Of nearly 2,000 responses to my RxS research, fewer than 1 percent reported stories that were positive, happy, or grateful of RxS that may or may not have led them to marry. To clarify: The data does not say that less than 1 percent of marriages that resulted from a Christian college are positive. Rather, less than 1 percent of responses to the survey indicated that students and graduates had positive reflections on the RxS culture (that is, the spoken or unspoken expectation to be married upon graduation). The culture of RxS is different from the act of becoming engaged or marrying in college. It would be difficult to decipher whether a couple got engaged because of the cultural expectation, or in spite of it, but we should not assume the pressure and the act are the same thing.

For the couples who met in college and married during or shortly after graduation, their relationship story was excused as an exception, which they seemed to recognize as ultimately negative. For example, one student reported:

> In a lot of ways I feel incredibly lucky to have ended up in such a solid, balanced, loving marriage. . . . I think we both realized that at twenty-three we were far from sure about anything, except that we loved each other and would make every attempt to grow in the same

> direction. But we have friends who rushed into marriage, and will likely be stuck in a relationship that doesn't work for a very long time.

The response above represents the one positive reflection or narrative, though it is still tinged with cautionary caveats. The implications of this are wide-ranging. It could suggest that those who benefited from the culture or became a stereotypical RxS couple are in denial or do not see how RxS was so detrimental to so many students and so do not feel the need to respond. Alternatively, it may suggest that RxS did not have any notable impact on student or alumni college experiences and is therefore not worthy of a response. I return to this issue in chapter 6 when I discuss the impact and implications of the culture, but the fact remains that the hurtful, damaging, and disparaging statistics and responses indicate that our duty as leaders in the Christian community requires honest reflection on how RxS culture affects college students today. The following chapters attempt to highlight this dynamic, and many others, to help us learn how to adequately address these issues in our respective institutions.

four

GENDERED NORMS

I came to college to focus on my career aspirations and for a love of learning. I had a romantic interest, but it wasn't reciprocated and I wasn't focused enough on ring by spring to make me desperate. It really bothered me when my friends would lament not having a boyfriend and how upset they got at not being "worthy" or pretty enough to be asked out. It made me worry that they would marry the first guy they dated. When I finally dated a guy starting at the end of my junior year, he was a friend first, but then got kind of crazy (he graduated several years before me from the same school). He became hyper-obsessed with marriage and me, making him the focus of my life, ahead of my first love, school. Our relationship was always headed toward marriage, from the moment we started dating. People around us got engaged, and friends of mine took extra classes to graduate early so they could become "wives." I remember hearing things like "the odds were really good for guys" because it was 60/40 female. . . . To summarize, I'd say that there were a lot of women defining their worth and goodness based on whether or not they had a boyfriend and that mostly it shaped the dating culture, you could only date one guy and it had to be with the ultimate goal of marriage.

THE DOMINANT NARRATIVE IN many evangelical Christian circles consists of a binary view of gender in which there are only two

41

genders—male and female—and that they are inherently different, with distinct social roles assigned by God. A "complementarian" view supports male-female sex and gender binary, and that these two sexes were created as counterparts that "complement" each other, though both are created in God's image. Other Protestant Christian circles have moved beyond a complementarian view of gender to recognize gender as a fluid concept, and to recognize the existence of intersex individuals—whose chromosomal, hormonal, or other genetic makeup do not biologically fit the two-sex model—who are also made in the image of God.

Still another perspective, a sociological one, contends that gender is a social construction with socially ascribed identities. Sociologists maintain that the roles men and women play in society derive from social pressures to perform in specific ways, rather than from natural or instinctual behaviors. The term "sex," on the other hand, is a strictly biological determination that is in itself problematic as a marker of identification, particularly those who identify biologically as intersex. The ways in which men, women, and other genders interact in society is therefore determinate entirely upon an individual's interpretation of what it means to be a man or woman.

Of course, there are grey areas in between these seemingly oppositional viewpoints. Nonetheless, regardless of one's perspective on sex and gender, the fact is that women and men have distinctive social experiences. The ongoing debate in the Christian church regarding gender roles, gender expectations, and the division of labor in the domestic sphere continues to rage, based on theological orientation and biblical interpretation. The ring by spring culture represents this tension in the church. Since the RxS ethos is built on the heteronormative expectation to find a mate and to marry, men and women are impacted differently. To begin, the phrase "ring by spring" itself suggests a woman's receipt of an engagement ring, thus implying that a woman is seeking a ring, thereby making the man in this context invisible. In traditional, heteronormative contexts, like at Christian colleges, when and how this happens is completely beyond the control of women; it is up to the man in the relationship to decide if and when the ring will appear. Men, therefore, are mostly in control of who becomes engaged in this context. The manner by which men and women respond to, and are influenced by, RxS is imperative to knowing how to work with young adults who find themselves entrenched in this culture.

This chapter explores the dynamics that shape the dating and relationship experiences of men and women on Christian college campuses, and it attempts to explain why women interact with RxS in a way that is fundamentally different from men. To begin, the social stigma associated with singlehood is different for men than it is for women. Men may choose to focus on their careers, for example, which is a more socially acceptable rationale for singlehood for men than women. For women, singleness may be interpreted by outsiders as the result of a personal issue that makes an individual undesirable. Women benefit from a marital social status, and are therefore more likely to pursue marriage.

Moreover, I argue that the dating marketplace at Christian colleges is skewed. There are more women than men at Christian colleges and universities, which contributes to the pressure that women feel to find a partner. Men, on the other hand, are at an advantage. Knowing that statistics are in their favor, some men may feel at liberty to date multiple women. Other men may choose not to date at all, believing that there will always be single Christian women available when they feel emotionally or financially prepared to marry. Since fewer men participate in organized religion than women, the dating marketplace for women seeking Christian men diminishes after graduation. For men, however, the dating marketplace continues to supply a high number of Christian women into mature adulthood. Thus, the pressure to find a spouse prior to graduation is much greater for women, as women may feel that the four years of college is their only opportunity to find a Christian husband. Consequently, the pressure is associated with a four-year ticking clock, which, combined with biologically related time-factors associated with fertility and reproduction, adds another dimension of stress that women are apt to feel.

43

The argument that follows is rooted in the heteronormative narrative that pervades Christian colleges and universities. In the following chapter, I will also describe how students that identify as lesbian, gay, bisexual, transgender, or queer (LGBTQ) may respond to and or interact with the RxS culture on campus, and will share how their experiences may differ from heterosexual couples in this context.

The Gendered Nature of Ring by Spring

In the first wave of my research with current students,[1] most respondents were women (82 percent), most were straight (90 percent), and most students considered themselves Protestant Christian (73 percent). When asked to write a definition for "ring by spring" *pressure* was the most often described word in their responses. When asked directly if they feel pressured to be married later in the survey, over two-thirds said they "definitely" felt or at least felt "a little bit" of pressure, though women were far more likely to report feeling pressured than men.[2]

		Definitely	A Little Bit	Not Really	Not at All	Already Married
Gender	Male	0	6 (22%)	12 (44%)	9 (33%)	0
	Female	16 (14.3%)	54 (50.1%)	20 (17.9%)	19 (17%)	3 (2.6%)
		14.3%	53.6%	28.9%	25%	2.6%

Table 4.1 Pressure to Marry by Gender

1. (n = 171) While this sample is just a portion of the university, and not necessarily representative of all CCCU student experiences, the results from this survey served as a launching point for future research in this topic.

2. Pressure to marry is generally higher for women than men, due to traditional social expectations of domesticity, but social pressures in addition to Christian pressures to refrain from sexual activity may generate a heightened sense of anxiety for women to be in a committed relationship. I will return to this and elaborate on the significance of gender in the following chapter.

Results from the survey reveal that, proportionally, women feel more pressure to be married during their time in college than do men. It is noteworthy that over eighty percent of the respondents in this study identify as female. This disproportionate[3] gender sample may indicate that women were more interested in communicating their experience than men. The pressure to marry in society in general is higher for women than men, due to traditional social expectations of domesticity, but social pressures in addition to Christian pressures to refrain from sexual activity may generate a heightened sense of anxiety for women to be in a committed relationship.

Social Pressures

The National Marriage Project, a research institute working out of the University of Virginia, conducted an extensive review of early marriages called "Knot Yet." They conducted a cost-benefit analysis of delaying marriages. In sum, they found that women tend to earn an average income of $18,000 dollars more if they delay marriage until their thirties. The assumption here is that women are more likely to focus on their jobs and careers before finding a spouse and having children, which is likely to upset income potential. The "Knot Yet" project also found that delaying marriage results in lower divorce rates. Not surprisingly, the more an individual has matured, become financially stable, and achieved a greater sense of self, the more stable the relationship.[4] So what is the rush to marry?

Singleness is often a greater anxiety-provoking social status for women than it is for men both inside and outside of Christian traditions. This can be largely attributed to three sources.[5] The first is that the social representation of the lady-in-waiting trope continues to thrive in society. We see representations of this caricature

3. The female population at the college is approximately 60 percent of the student population

4. Hymowitz et al., "Knot Yet."

5. Lahad, "Singlehood."

all over the media (cue romantic comedy formula of single woman pressured to find a partner meets goofy, lovable single man without such pressure), and clichés such as "always a bridesmaid, never a bride," assuming that a single woman is always waiting next in line to move forward in life as a married woman. The assumption is that marriage is the goal, and remaining single represents a woman's inability to achieve that status.

The second reason is that single women are often perceived to be in a liminal period, passively waiting for the so-called Prince Charming to come and sweep them off their feet. A woman that chooses to be single—either indefinitely, or at a certain stage in her life—is perceived to be unwanted, even undesirable. Regardless of whether she chooses to be single, the dominant cultural narrative remains that women are expected to wait for a man rather than pursue a relationship on her own. Conversely, men are assumed to be the actors in romantic relationships; they are in charge of whether or not they are in a relationship, so their singleness status is unquestioned or unjudged by society. As a result, the man who is unmarried is not waiting to be chosen. Society might excuse him from marrying for holding high standards, or being focused on his career, or being content with himself so he does not need a partner.

Third, the premarital anticipation of single women is in contrast to other social pressures associated with age: the pressure of biological clocks and the threat of becoming an "old maid."[6] For some, the proverbial biological clock pressures women to rush to marry and to have children before they reach a certain age and their fertility drops. Having children or achieving motherhood is a subsequent cultural requisite that comes after fulfilling the gendered social expectation to marry. Finding a spouse, and finding a spouse young when women are in their reproductive prime, can be a genuine concern for those women who dream of starting families through their own reproductive means. In general, men do not feel the same pressure to become fathers, nor is their fecundity questioned when they reach a certain age without having had children.

6. Lahad, "Singlehood," 166.

To accentuate the complicated gender dynamics women navigate in contemporary US society, the Christian church also maintains a complex relationship with women. Biblical representations of womanhood are often limited to mother-like figures, such as the Virgin Mary, or harlots such as Rahab or Mary Magdalene (who both repent and become followers). This sends a message to women and girls that they must strive to be like the virgin mother (which becomes reproductively complicated) in order to be honorable. The woman in Prov 31 is also often cited as being representative of true biblical womanhood and is referred to as "The Wife of Noble Character." This scriptural passage is almost always referenced to women, for women, and about women. However, verse 31 reads, "Praise her for all her hands have done," implying that the chapter is actually directed toward men, expecting men to appreciate the work of women. So why act as though this impossibly demanding checklist is a duty for women? These gendered narratives may not be explicitly stated on Sunday mornings (though sometimes they are), but the message becomes internalized, and results in women feeling they must be with a man in order to be considered valuable.

Dating Marketplace

Social exchange theory provides a perspective that may be useful for explaining why students may get married during college. To begin, social exchange theory suggests that social behavior, including mate selection, is the result of an exchange process whereby any social exchange is meant to maximize benefits and minimize costs. According to this theory, people weigh the potential benefits and risks or "costs" of relationships, seeking to find relationships that only provide benefits or social "rewards." For women, the rewards associated with engagement and marriage far outweigh the costs, including social status in society and among their peers, personal goals, religious affirmation, and university culture. For Christian women, however, the costs of singleness are too high, and the benefits or rewards of early marriage are so robust, that it is rational for women to want to find their mate and become engaged prior to graduation.

According to social psychologists, relationships grow, develop, deteriorate, and dissolve as a consequence of social exchanges. When we interact with others, we are constantly negotiating the costs and benefits of our relationships with others.[7] That is, both men and women weigh the costs and benefits of participating in, and committing to, intimate relationships. If men do not see value in the social rewards that come from marriage (status, for example), then their interest in developing deep relationships with women may not be as high. As a result, women are not only more directly impacted by RxS, but their motive is greater, making an unequal balance in those seeking and not seeking engagement and marriage in college. This disequilibrium plays a considerable role in the added stress or pressure in the dating marketplace at Christian colleges.

Single women are exposed to greater social pressures to be married than are men both in the Christian community and in society. The pressure intensifies when women reach emerging adulthood, and are in the company of other Christians in an environment where marriage is perceived as the norm. For example, for a young woman who comes from a traditional background that instructs her to marry a Christian man, the expectation to marry while in early adulthood (college age) is implicit, if not explicitly stated, given the traditional gender roles prescribed by conservative Christian backgrounds. These families may assume that there is no better place to find a Christian man than at a Christian college, where Christian men and women are studying, living, and worshiping together. It sounds like a perfect place to find and meet a spouse. And some do! When they do, their union is praised when those couples are confident in their mate selection process and feel adequately prepared for marriage. However, some students do not graduate with a spouse, which leads some women to think that they failed at their college experience, that they missed their

---

7. Thibaut and Kelley, *Social Psychology of Groups*.

opportunity to claim a husband from a large selection of young available Christian men.

To contribute to this pressure, college women must also navigate a world where the "supply" of potential male partners is disproportionately low. Christian colleges attract more female students than they do male students. This is due to a number of reasons: First, Christianity tends to attract more women than men, and religious affiliation is often a determining factor of why students select Christian colleges. Second, parents may be more inclined to encourage their daughters to attend a Christian college, which is perceived as safer than a large, public university where women may be perceived as more vulnerable. Finally, across the country, liberal arts universities—whether or not they are religiously affiliated—tend to be more attractive to female students given the academic programs available, as well as the perception to be more connected with a community (a variable that women appear to find more appealing than men).

A number of women students and alum admitted feeling the need to prove to be the best Christian woman, so she could attract the best Christian man. For example, one alum wrote:

> We (as women) were there to find a good Christian man-spouse and if you were just dating to date, you were on the wrong path. Dating was reserved for leading to marriage and if you couldn't tie a guy down, you failed at RxS, and as a Christian woman there was something a little wrong with you. Basically, the pressure to be the "right" kind of Christian woman that would be desirable to a "man of God."

The result may be increased competition among women in a race to find the marriageable men among the population. Since dating casually is unusual on Christian college campuses, the only way to find a partner is to be the most attractive woman on the outside, pitting woman against woman in the pursuit of a partner. If the dating norm at Christian college involves following the courtship model—where only serious relationships form after a man has decided that the woman he is attracted to is worthy of being pursued—then a woman must present herself in a way that is superficially attractive. Thus, women are likely to feel more pressure to look a certain way, act a certain way, and behave as close to their perceptions of what a "Christian woman" is supposed to be, which may result in a disingenuous self-portrayal rather than being true to her own identity. Thus, the women are competing against each other to be the most attractive candidate to the Christian men that are looking for a spouse. As a result, if a woman is not courted, she may feel she is unworthy due to her looks, self-presentation, or other shallow indicators of identity.

This competition did not seem to end once a relationship was formed. Some students commented that the competition did not end until the woman got her engagement ring. Up until that point, the man in the relationships could still decide to date other women on campus. Hence, the rush and pressure to become engaged to secure that relationship. One female respondent from the alumni survey reported:

> Most men at a Christian college who want to date are looking for a wife. Most women who want to date are looking for a husband. So I was pursued as wife-material, and was also told if I didn't "hurry it up" I'd face competition with the guy I was dating, who was apparently husband material.

As a result, women may become panicked, desperate, to attract a man, date, and marry before graduation, after which her opportunities to attract Christian men would diminish.

The Four-Year Window

Given that Christian colleges are predominantly female, often representing 60 percent or more of the student population, women are at a disadvantage for finding a straight male partner. Assuming a heteronormative culture on these college campuses, the male-to-female ratio is so skewed that straight women have a limited dating pool. Suffice it to say, at Christian universities, men hold the advantage when it comes to finding a spouse. Not only are women more likely to be searching for a prospective mate, but there are *more* women than men, making the available dating pool nearly twice as large for men as for women, in some cases. As a result, the pressure to find a romantic partner may be less intensive for men, since it is not as competitive to find one of the available women before they are betrothed to someone else.

One of the repeated themes heard when Christian college students and alum discussed RxS is their fear that they would not find a good match after they had left college. After all, in what other context would students be surrounded by like-minded men and women who share their Christian values? The four-year clock to meet and marry someone while in this context seems especially stressful. Students and alum commented on this dynamic:

> I feel like there was an expectation that I should have found the person I was going to marry in college. The fact that I didn't has made dating harder after graduation. Like, what if I missed my opportunity?

> [Ring by spring] normalized the idea that it was good to get engaged by the end of college; put pressure on me to date in college, with the idea that if I didn't find a spouse in college, I wouldn't find one later in life.

> I think many people hope to find their future spouse in college because you have many opportunities to socialize and meet with new people, and people fear that they will suddenly lose access to the huge pool of opportunity upon graduation. However, when I graduated, I realized that this idea was a complete myth! I was not cut off from the pool of opportunity; in fact, I found it easier to devote more time to socialization when I no longer had mountains of homework hanging over my head at all times. It was liberating.

I would argue that it is this clock that contributes to the pressure for women. For men, becoming engaged in college is not necessarily a benefit with the same package of social rewards, so the four-year clock does not cause as much concern.

Relationships Across Genders

As previously reported, most men do not experience the same amount of pressure that is reported by women. One male respondent, when explaining why he chose not to date, stated: "It puts a lot of pressure on men to date women. The women all fight over the same guys and act desperate for love. I think the relationship feels constantly pressured." Rather than considering how a serious relationship could potentially be rewarding for this man, he had no hesitation in reporting that marriage during college was not an initial goal.

Another male alum response indicated that if men did date, there is an underlying pressure to make it very serious from the outset. According to him:

> I do think it's appropriate to say that the [ring by spring] cultural expectation may have impacted my dating experience in a sense. I always assumed that my female partners wanted to sort out, rather quickly, whether or not the relationship would lead to marriage . . . and I think that I was always trying to figure that out far too soon, rather than just being "mindful" and present and seeing what developed. I think that I often felt that if I didn't end up marrying someone, I had wronged them in a really significant way.

This dynamic did not only affect men; some women also suggested that the serious nature of relationships during college made it challenging to have friendships that were strictly platonic. One alum wrote:

> By framing relationships with men as primarily potential husbands, I think the culture made it very difficult for me to have deep male-female friendships or even act naturally with single young men—and these are things that I still struggle with. I think it also made me feel like

a hopeless spinster in my early-twenties because so many of my friends had already married/had kids, whereas in contrast my [current] friends are just now (in their mid-thirties) marrying. I haven't dated much at all, and I think that's been in part reaction to (rebelling against) the weird gender dynamics I experienced and in part because of my awkwardness with men.

According to Pew Research's "Religious Landscape Survey," women outnumber men in every Protestant Christian tradition.[8] Consequently, straight Christian men could easily select a mate given the selection of women available. The outcome is that men may believe that they have the freedom to "shop around" and find their best match based on the process of elimination even after the four year college experience ends. For women, they may be more interested in finding available Christian men, and so put more pressure on each individual relationship to make sure that it sticks.

The concept of "relational maximization" may provide a helpful frame through which we understand the gender dynamics associated with the RxS phenomenon. Relational maximization refers to the desire to find (and to be in a relationship with) the best partner.[9] The role of maximization in the formation, development, and even dissolution of romantic relationships implies that some individuals would be more likely to look for "the best" romantic partner instead of one who would be "good enough." A "satisfi-cer" would be those who do not seek maximization; instead they become "satisfied" with the best available choice, as long as that choice meets a set of basic criteria. Therefore, how people make decisions in romantic relationships directly relates to their levels of satisfaction, investment, and commitment in the relationship.[10]

The relational maximization frame suggests that because straight women have a smaller pool of potential mates, women are more likely to be satisficers. Being satisfied in their romantic partners if he meets the minimum standard for some: a Christian

8. Pew Research Center, "Religious Landscape."

9. Mikkelson, Hesse, and Pauley, "Attributes," 567.

10. Mikkelson and Pauley, "Maximizing."

man. The pressure associated with finding a spouse is so great that finding a partner may become the primary goal for some, rather than attempting to maximize his or her full potential. Contrary to this, men may take their pick of women, knowing that the relationship pool is in their favor. Therefore, men may become more relational maximizers and therefore do not feel pressure on the same level that women do. Men may choose not to date without experiencing the four-year ticking clock to find a spouse, they likely do not need to modify their self-presentation in order to be courted since Christian men are typically the pursuers, and they may not have the social and biological pressures to begin a family in the same way women do. As a result, the dating marketplace becomes constrained, where those in demand are not as available as the relationship seekers would like to assume. One student wrote:

> Women more than men (although not strictly) feel more pressure to meet someone and have a deep relationship relatively quickly. I have had girlfriends that have gone through periods of not dating and have felt lonely and unloved and unsought, although they were perfectly lovely and unique and spirited. There is almost an air of "if you aren't in a relationship you are not meaningful" and I wish that people would just focus on their lives and paths, because desperation is not attractive. Men, I feel, play the game a little more and want to test the field before getting too serious.

The impact of this gender dynamic has serious consequences for relationships of all types. Friendships and romantic relationships alike are put under the microscope as individuals try to guess the others' intentions in the first days or weeks of their relationship. One alum admitted that maintaining male friendships during and after her time at a Christian college proved to be difficult. Friendships across gender lines are important for establishing healthy relationships without questioning the romantic or sexual interest of the other party. Another alum recalled the challenge of making male friendships in an environment where male-female relationships are always under the social microscope. She wrote:

I think my lack of male friendships are a result of the competitive atmosphere was unfortunate and made me continue to be shy and rather awkward with men, rather than getting over that and figuring out how to relate to men in a primarily non-romantic way. I am a fairly easily embarrassed person, so I feel the Christian dating culture in combination with that personality trait has rather hampered my relationships with men.

Another alum wrote:

It was quite difficult to make guy friends because the girls were very competitive about their male friends (usually harboring hopes that it would eventually become romantic) and you had to be quite aggressive/assertive in order to become friends with guys, since because of the gender imbalance they had as many female friends as they could wish. My friends and I jokingly called the female groups that often developed around a particular guy their harem, because they would often act that way in terms being very attentive in providing for the guy's needs (back rubs, emotional support, giving ego boosts by their sort of fawning attention that was not reciprocated). Since I wasn't willing to play that game I had almost no male friends by the time I graduated university.

These comments represent the voice of many students trying to explain the complicated gender dynamics prevalent on college campuses. While some may argue that dating in general is a "high risk, high reward" endeavor, for those at a Christian college that may be a risk some men (or women) are unwilling to take. The following conversation took place in a focus group conducted by a purposive sample of students representing a variety of races, genders, religious and sexual orientations, and ages. What follows is an example of how students perceive the complicated dynamics between men and women on campus:

Kimberly: I've heard people say, "oh, there aren't many guys and the good ones are already taken. That's very common in the girl culture here. So I wonder what the guys think, assuming heterosexuality.

Emma: Like, no rush.

Kimberly: Yeah. Like, "They're just trying to trap me!" Or maybe that's just a bro-joke?

Aaron: So are you saying basically that the greater the scarcity of options, the greater the amplification of pressure for women?

Kimberly: Right. Yes. Exactly.

Aaron: So maybe that's even greater for LGBT people.

Kimberly: Oh, I was just going to talk about that!

Kimberly and I will talk about that in detail in the next chapter.

Conclusion

Men and women interact with the RxS culture in very distinct ways. Women are often the subject of the RxS discussion, yet men are clearly involved in dating relationships as well, since most students at Christian colleges identify as straight and pursue male-female relationships. The experiences facing straight women differ from those women who identify as lesbian, for example. Thus, the gender binary described in this chapter is best understood in the context of normative man-woman straight relationships, which are the most prominent at Christian colleges. In addition to discussing Christian views of sex, the following chapter addresses how same-sex relationships, and other dimensions of sexuality, may be impacted by Christian college students' perspectives on dating and marriage.

five

SEX AND SEXUALITY

> Having sex before marriage was so far out of the ques-
> tion, that it certainly expedited marriage for several of
> my friends. I think the fact that we were not concerned
> about whether or not our church thought we should have
> sex gave us more reason to wait to marry until we were
> actually ready.

IF THE CHRISTIAN CHURCH has an uncomfortable relationship
with gender, its relationship with sex and sexuality is even more
difficult. The *status quo* in most Christian circles is to avoid the
topic all together, while presuming sex is practiced only in the
confines of marriage. Thus, when people think about ring by
spring, or Christian dating culture in general, many assume the
pressure Christians feel to marry their partner quickly stems from
their desire to have sex within the context of marriage. Since most
traditional Christian traditions insist on abstinence outside of
marriage, the only way for Christians to experience their sexuality
without feeling "sinful" is to marry. Despite popular belief, some
students at Christian colleges are having sex outside of marriage
anyway, and the pressure to find a spouse exists even for sexually
active students.

Religious affiliation only partially explains student sexual behavior, thus it is inadequate to assume the pressure to marry that
comes from RxS cannot be reduced to sex. While some students,

57

Christian or non-Christian, may want to remain abstinent until marriage, others may not. The RxS surveys did not produce any conclusive data to suggest that student pressures to marry young are correlated with their desire to have sex in the context of marriage. In fact, the student survey responses indicate that Christian college students are having sex, regardless of marital status or strict university policies that prohibit sexual relationships on campus. Essentially, those students who want to have sex will and do, and those that wish to remain abstinent do. I asked students in the first survey whether they have ever been sexually active (according to their definition of "sex"). One third (33.5 percent) said yes, one third said no (33.8 percent) and another third chose not to answer the question. Thus, RxS is more complicated than the pressure to have sex.

This chapter explores sexuality in two ways. First, I briefly review how sex is perceived in Christianity. The various interpretations of scripture lead to drastically different policies and perspectives on how we should approach sex and sexuality in Christian circles (including at Christian colleges). I also explain how the cultural dimensions of ring by spring—a quintessentially heteronormative complex—apply to the LGBTQ student community at Christian colleges. Moreover, given the wide variation of experiences expressed, I also explore the relationship dynamics described by students at one particular college. The stories they shared, and the concerns they raised, are invaluable for recognizing the variety of ways in which institutional dating culture can affect relationships—gay or straight—among Christian college students. Due to the limited access of students identifying as bisexual, transgender, intersex, or asexual, this study cannot speak fully to those students' experiences on campus.

Sex and Christianity

There is not one, single Christian perspective on sex and sexuality; not all Christians share the same beliefs about sex and sexuality. There are multiple perspectives on sexuality in the Bible that cause

conflict and confusion in the Christian community. The most common and more traditional perspective is that Christians should
remain abstinent until marriage. This particular idea is rooted in
what I call the "one flesh"[1] perspective. The term "one flesh" is first
seen in the Bible in Gen 2:24. Here, God is in the process of creating Adam and Eve and asserts: "Therefore a man leaves his father
and his mother and clings to his wife, and they become one flesh."[2]
The subsequent conclusions made by many theologians, therefore,
is that sex creates an inseparable bond that should only occur
within the context of marriage. Other scriptural passages reference adulterers, including the seventh commandment, "You shall
not commit adultery." The New Revised Standard Version uses the
word "adultery" forty-two times, condemning such behavior. This
includes even lustful thoughts that may cause sexual arousal and
impure thoughts or intentions.[3]

There is no doubt that Christian scriptures suggest we control our sexual urges and desires. Thus, the dominant Christian
perspective requires that individuals need to "save themselves" or
"remain pure" or refrain from any sexual activity until they are
married. At this point, everything changes, and men and women
are expected to have sex often, and to enjoy it. The Message paraphrases Paul's recommendations of marital sexuality in 1 Cor
7:1–6:

> Now, getting down to the questions you asked in your
> letter to me. First, is it a good thing to have sexual rela-
> tions? Certainly—but only within a certain context. It's
> good for a man to have a wife, and for a woman to have a
> husband. Sexual drives are strong, but marriage is strong
> enough to contain them and provide for a balanced and
> fulfilling sexual life in a world of sexual disorder. The
> marriage bed must be a place of mutuality—the husband
> seeking to satisfy his wife, the wife seeking to satisfy
> her husband. Marriage is not a place to "stand up for

1. Gen 2:24; Matt 19:5; Mark 10:8; Eph 5:31.

2. New Revised Standard Version.

3. "But I say to you that everyone who looks at a woman with lust has
already committed adultery with her in his heart" (Matt 5:28, NRSV).

your rights." Marriage is a decision to serve the other, whether in bed or out. Abstaining from sex is permissible for a period of time if you both agree to it, and if it's for the purposes of prayer and fasting—but only for such times. Then come back together again. Satan has an ingenious way of tempting us when we least expect it. I'm not, understand, commanding these periods of abstinence—only providing my best counsel if you should choose them.

Another, less prevalent perspective of sex that is adopted by some Christians is that God cares less about social constructs of sex, and more about living our lives in ways that honor God and follow Christ. This includes not idolizing sex or participating in immoral sexual behaviors. Idolizing sex may manifest in a virgin's obsession with refraining from sex. In this case, sexual abstinence remains the focus on one's daily living, and is the central focus on relationships. If sex becomes so central in a relationship, couples may rush to marry in order to avoid the sin that they associate with premarital sex. Instead, this theology of scripture maintains that a healthy, consensual sexual relationship can be honorable and pleasing to God.

Recognizing the spiritual purpose of sexuality is an important step in understanding its place in relationships. Debra Hirsch writes in her book, *Redeeming Sex*:

> If we are created in the image of God, then our sexuality reflects something of who God is. Sex is not just a means to the end of the propagation of the species, or even for fun, but to make the Creator known.[4]

The purpose of this chapter is not to argue for or against one particular interpretation of scriptural references to sex and sexuality. What I hope to point out is that there are multiple perspectives to understanding sexuality in a Christian context, and that suggesting that Christians do not have sex outside of marriage is not only inaccurate, but it also assumes that Christians do not carry

4. Hirsch, *Redeeming Sex*, 29.

different opinions about how God views sexuality. As Dianna Anderson writes:

> God's plan for sexuality has many facets. A sexual relationship with your partner, married or not, committed for life or not. We bring our own sacredness into our sexual lives, imparting our own meanings to the relationship. Some of these meanings we derive from Scripture. Others we get from our life experiences, and still others from what we discuss with our partners. Our sexual lives do not have only one meaning—they are instead a beautiful amalgamation of the facets of two different lives. These varied meanings are developed regardless of marital status.[5]

There are many resources that critique sex and Christian theology. To summarize all of them would distract from the central focus of this study, which is the impact of young marriages on other students. However, it is important to note that commentators repeatedly suggest that RxS and the pressure to marry young is due to pressure evangelical Christian culture places on youth to remain abstinent before marriage. This pressure is felt by both men and women; men are discouraged from having any sexual impulses[6] and women are shamed if they have sexual impulses or engage in any sexual activity that would challenge their virginity or "purity."[7]

For those students who choose to be sexually active, Christian college policies and campus conversations have a clear message about the topic: just don't. Most Christian colleges have rules that enforce gender segregation during sleeping hours. That is, there are no co-educational or cross-listed dormitory floors, there are typically "visitation hours" during which men are not allowed on women's floors and vice versa. The purpose of these regulations is to prevent sexual activity in student housing. Malone, author of *From Single to Serious*, writes:

5. Anderson, *Damaged Goods*, 59.

6. Diefendorf, "After."

7. Malone, *From Single to Serious*; Regenerus and Eucker, *Premarital Sex*; Frietas, *Sex and the Soul*.

The principle behind these rules is clearly at odds with the "no-strings-attached" nature of hooking up. In addition, most hookups occur after students have consumed some amount of alcohol, and/or spent time together at a party or in their (coed) residence hall. Since most evangelical schools do not permit alcohol consumption or have coeducational residence halls, their campus environment does not encourage such encounters. Thus, the campus context is a key component in understanding the ways in which intimate relationships, gender, and sexuality are mobilized on campus.[8]

What is more, these rules often overlook same-sex relationships, bisexual, or transgender students. By overlooking the possibility that these students do live and exist on college campuses, lesbian, gay, bisexual, transgender, and queer (LGBTQ) student identities are therefore disregarded, a topic I return to in a few pages.

Ultimately, traditional Christian values surrounding gender identity and sexuality are rooted in theological understandings of sexual purity until marriage. Purity culture discourages physical contact, and certainly discourages any romantic activities at all with members of the same sex or gender. One alum responded:

> My perception of sex as a dirty and dangerous activity was fostered during my college experience. The "hush, hush" forbidden nature of it added to my anxiety and fear.

Whether or not sex is prohibited on campus, the impact of keeping sex off the table for discussion has long-term effects on Christian men and women.[9] One student reflected, "When it comes to sex, they [the staff at Christian colleges] assume you're either married, or you're committed to never having sex. Ever."

A study on evangelical men and sexuality should be an important reference for those working with Christian men and women who adhere to an abstinent lifestyle outside of marriage.

8. Malone, *From Single to Serious*, 190.
9. Diefendorf, "After."

In this study, the author describes a support group for evangelical men to share their concerns about sexuality prior to marriage. After marriage, however, men continue to struggle with sexuality but are not supported in the same way once they are married. They find themselves alone in their concerns about their sexuality and judged by those in religious institutions (including their Christian wives). As a result, this could inhibit a healthy sex life for future marriages. The author writes:

> This highly gendered, highly contextualized understanding of sexuality as beastly, wonderful, promised, and unfulfilled requires years of pre-marriage conversation, and although not offered, seems to require the same after marriage. While the tensions between both sacred and beastly discourses require a constant and open dialogue about sex before marriage, the inability to balance the tension between these discourses in married life leave these men unprepared for the sexual lives for which they have spent so much time preparing.[10]

In her study of Christian college relationship rituals, Malone found that Christian college women do not see or interpret sexuality as something for the present moment or something that is part of their lives now. The "forbidden sex" message has run so deep, that the possibility in engaging in it seems so far off—especially if the student is not currently dating someone they intend to marry. For these students, sex may not be considered a reason to rush in.

Sex and Ring by Spring

Returning to the topic of RxS, I wanted to explore whether sex really is the ultimate source of the pressure students may feel to marry young. I asked students to share whether they felt pressured to have sex while at a Christian school. Two-thirds of students (63.3 percent) responded with "not really" or "not at all," while 27 percent of students said "a little" and only 9 percent said "definitely." In

10. Diefendorf, "After," 666.

comparison to the pressure students reported regarding marriage or engagement, the pressure to have sex is much lower, thereby assuming that sex isn't as much of a factor in the engagement process as perhaps other scholars have ventured to presume.

Furthermore, when asked directly whether students had ever been sexually active, based on their own interpretation of sex asked in a previous question, their responses failed to indicate any clear patterns of behavior: students were having sex whether or not they attended church. While the data reveal that students who do attend church are more likely to refrain from sexual activity, it may not deter others.

Table 5.1 Church Attendance and Sexual Activity

How often do you attend church?		Are you, or have you ever been, sexually active?	
		Yes	No
	Never	8%	1.5%
	Once or twice a year	7%	1.5%
	A few times a year	9%	3%
	Once a month	5%	10%
	Once a week	17%	18%
	At least once a week	6%	15%
	Total	52%	49%

Joel Willits, professor of biblical and theological studies at a Christian university outside of Chicago, claims to have "good sense of what Christian college students think about sex." He writes in his blog:

> Only a very small minority of students think sex should be saved for marriage. It is clear that this message is what parents have taught them, but they neither follow that advice nor do they think it is what Jesus asks of them these days. . . . Students think sex within a committed, loving,

and protective relationship is acceptable to Jesus, even if it is not exclusively within a marriage relationship.[11]

This book is not about sexuality and Christianity directly. There are many books dedicated strictly to this topic that are worth reading and considering. While I do not think the pressure to remain abstinent until marriage (the foundation of what is known as the purity culture) is an insignificant contribution to the conversation around RxS (in fact, I see it is a central factor to many Christian relationships), I do not think it is the only explanation that drives young people to marry young. Blaming young Christian marriages on the purity culture primarily is a unidimensional explanation of relationships in Christian settings. While the evidence clearly suggests that evangelical Christianity's stress on sexual purity does lead Christian men and women to marry earlier than the national average, it is by no means the only reason students seek marital partners at Christian colleges. The truth is, Christian college students—particularly women—feel pressured to marry whether or not they are have having sex with their partners. RxS is more than a manifestation of purity culture; it is a post-purity cultural phenomenon that appears to affect Christians and non-Christians, those who believe in sexual purity and those who do not.

Sexuality and the Experiences of LGBTQ Students

As argued in the previous chapter, the pressure to marry varies greatly across gendered groups, where women appear to experience more pressure than men. This trend remains true among LGBTQ students, where lesbians feel pressure to be in serious relationships, despite their non-normative sexual orientation. Therefore, only heterosexual relationships are the norm at Christian colleges, but traditional relationship rules still appear to apply to all students regardless of their sexual preferences. Same-sex relationships violate those norms, yet it would be remiss to ignore the

11. Willits, "What," para. 4.

growing LGBTQ (lesbian, gay, bisexual, transgender, queer, inter-sex, asexual) student population in the United States and indeed at Christian colleges. One student reported:

> I don't know that I can generalize this necessarily to other gay men, or to any other demographic, really, but I feel fairly removed from the stereotype of RxS. I never had anyone ask when I was dating, "When are you guys getting married?" I've never felt pressured in that with my friends, so I always felt outside of that narrative of RxS. I mean, I haven't felt pressured internally, or by other people to be part of the RxS culture.

As this student shared, just because the dating patterns these students experience are outside the cultural norm, does not mean that dating and relationship pressures are absent from their Christian college experience. Their relationships, however, do look differently than the heterosexual relationships in their midst.

LGBTQ Student Population

The challenges that LGBTQ students on Christian campuses face is understudied and mostly unknown to public audiences.[12] Despite the 2013 Supreme Court decision to eradicate the Defense of Marriage Act (DOMA), there are only a few CCCU schools that are open and affirming to the LGBTQ community, creating a conflicting and confusing dynamic for students identifying as members of this population. *The Atlantic* published an article in 2016 that describes how LGBTQ students' experiences can be a challenge at CCCU schools:

> In the past, many conservative Christian colleges con-demned both same-sex attraction and same-sex inti-macy. But now that same-sex marriage is legalized, and as the country undergoes broad cultural shifts, that's changing. Some of these same schools are now attempt-ing to separate sexual identity from sexual behavior in their policies and campus customs. However awkwardly,

12. Coley, *Gay on God's Campus.*

they are trying to welcome gay students while preserving rules against same-sex "behavior."[13]

The Council for Christian Colleges and University's standard for LGBTQ students, faculty, and staff is complicated to say the least. In 2016, the CCCU created categories of institutional involvement based on whether the institution recognizes and affirms same-sex relationships. Those that explicitly state opposition to non-heteronormative relationships are those considered to be full members of the CCCU and are granted governing rights as well as priority to grants and other institutional incentives.

The degree of openness to LGBTQ students varies widely at CCCU institutions. According to one database of 682 Christian colleges and universities in the United States, about 45 percent of the schools had approved LGBTQ groups, and 55 percent had adopted statements of nondiscrimination based on sexual orientation.[14] As a result, it is difficult to adequately measure the degree to which LGBTQ students were impacted by RxS. It is possible, if not likely, that there are alumni that remained closeted during college because of the relationship norms that existed on campus. Same-sex relationships may or may not have been allowed by university student conduct codes. Some alumni graduated college during a time when the same-sex marriages were not recognized, and therefore were unable to participate in marriage, let alone engage with the RxS culture. These considerations are worthy of an entire study of its own! The complicated nature of the relationship between LGBTQ students and Christian college culture makes it challenging to adequately address their relationship experiences during college. Nonetheless, what I report below are initial exploratory inquiries into the experiences of some LGBTQ students at CCCU schools and how their exposure to dating may differ from straight students on campus.

13. Wheeler, "LGBTQ Politics," para. 1.
14. Coley, *Gay on God's Campus.*

LGBTQ Student Perspectives

While it is possible for LGBTQ students to get their ring by spring, it is not necessarily culturally acceptable on a Christian college campus. Whether Christian institutions ought to adopt these social standards is beyond the scope of my research. For this study, I wish to focus on whether LGBTQ students experience the same pressure to marry as straight students. Responses to the alumni survey included seventy-four members from the LGBTQ community. The responses do not exhibit any prominent trends (see Table 5.2 below), making it difficult to summarize the experiences of those who responded to the survey. However, the qualitative responses from alumni and the focus groups conducted with LGBTQ students do provide an important—and often overlooked—lens on the experiences of LGBTQ students at Christian colleges.

Table 5.2 LGBT Students and Pressure to Marry During College

	Frequency	Percent
Definitely	8	9%
A little bit	28	31.5%
Not really	22	24.7%
Not at all	30	33.7%
I was already married	1	1.1%

Results from the survey responses revealed a high awareness of ring by spring while at college, but a low rate of participation in the culture. When asked to define RxS in their own words, five respondents described it using pejorative language such as "ludicrous," "silly," or "idiotic." Five responses described RxS as either a "heteronormative myth" or a "social construct." Three responses included a mention of RxS as an antiquated or old "tradition." Four respondents stated that college had negatively impacted, "jaded," or "sour[ed]" their perception of marriage.

Of the seventy-four alumni respondents, however, only four mentioned feeling outright discriminated against as an LGBTQ student during their college years. One respondent recalled:

> I was vilified and shunned by faculty (notably, my advisor), other students, and health center doctors. They taught me that I was outside God's love, and would never marry.

Lastly, when asked to describe their feelings about being single at graduation twenty-three respondents (32 percent of the sample) reported feeling "fine." Ten felt "good" or "great," and three reported finding a sense of "freedom" in their relationship status. Others, however, mentioned feeling "left out" or "excluded" from such a unifying tradition, and only two felt "judged" by their peers for failing to fulfill RxS.

When asked to describe how college changed their understanding of marriage, responses also varied widely. Below are a few examples:

> My time at college caused me to think regularly about what my future was to look like and the idea of being married was put on a pedestal.

> I came into college believing that, as a gay Christian, I would never marry. I left college with every intention of finding and marrying a man someday.

> College showed me that conservative, white Christians tend to have a narrowly heterosexual/binary-gender leaning idea of sexuality and partnership, the sacred union of marriage, and what it means to be in a relationship.

The range of LGBTQ student responses was so broad, and the social contexts so variable, that it remains clear that more research is necessary to better understand their experiences at Christian colleges. Consequently, in order to capture how students in 2018 approach dating I coordinated focus groups conducted on one Christian college campus. These students were purposely selected to participate in the group to provide a diverse perspective on these relational dynamics.

LGBTQ Students Speak Out

The narratives below reflect how students identifying as gay or lesbian—a clear minority on campus—navigate dating on campus, let alone discussions of engagement and marriage dictated by RxS culture norms. One student approached the topic saying:

> At a Christian school, too, it's like [*sheepishly*], "Are you gay? Like, I think there's something here, but maybe you're just really friendly." I mean, how do you even navigate those conversations? So there is just so many different layers to LGBTQ dating here [at this Christian college].

> I am a lesbian, a senior, and I've been in three relationships since I got to college. . . . I definitely felt the relationship pressure when I got here. I mean, I thought, "Okay, there's like two gay people." Like what options did I have? I thought, "Okay, there are only four of you, so I've got to pick right!" It's definitely like an LGBT thing here where if you date someone, the next person probably hooked up with them as well. So there's this very small web. So once you date one, if you break up you're screwed because you probably have the same friend group. Or you have similar networks. So I felt very pressured to stay in that relationship because if we break up, I have no other options.

> I think that the ring by spring is that so little options is that there is the pressure that, "Oh, this is it. This is all I have!" Dating is sparse, but for me, I never felt it tied into ring by spring. I didn't feel pressured and I never felt like other people pressured me. My interpretation is that I

didn't fit the mold of ring by spring so they didn't put that
on me, because it wasn't *their* understanding of ring by
spring. You know, straight versus gay relationships.

The lesbian experience differs from the experience of gay
men in this context. One male respondent identifying as gay wrote
in the alumni survey.

As a closeted gay man, I did feel pressure from others to
date women, but I was able to brush it off because I was
so active in school.

Would women—including lesbian or bisexual women—have
the ability to brush it off the same way this man could? I would
venture to guess that the web of oppression is such that social
norms about women in relationships interacting with conservative
or traditional cultures results in women continuing to feel pressure
to be in a relationship.

Kimberly shared more of her experience that supports this
hypothesis:

There's the stereotype "U-Haul lesbian" that on the second date you move in together. So it's like the stereotype
that lesbians are very homey. Like, "let's date and then
get married tomorrow." I definitely got a lot of that. Like,
people asking if I am living with my girlfriend. I mean so
many people, "Well, are you going to move in together?"
I'm like, "No, I'm living with a friend!" But it's just assumed that I'm going to move in with my girlfriend.
Like, immediately. So that makes me wonder if it's more
about gender, then. That women feel like it's that pressure, regardless of sexuality. And it's more of a gender
thing.

Despite her sexual preference, her college peers still expected
Kimberly to enter a serious relationship with her girlfriend, presumably to continue to uphold gendered standards that expect
women to be in a relationship, even if their relationship is with
another woman. The implications of this discovery require much

more research and investigation into the experiences of LGBTQ individuals in Christian environments.

Relationships of All Types Matter

The desire for intimate relationships is about more than just sexual intimacy. In chapter 2, I described the environment of some Christian colleges that foster—if not force—intentional relationships on the students. It is the culture of the university, reinforced by the adopted culture of the students, to be serious, intentional, and to "go deep" in their relationships with others. No relationships are trivial, including dating relationships. The impact of this ethos has greater implications on the lives of Christian college students than is intended.

The narrative that male-female romantic relationships are the only romantic relationships to occur on campus is not only flawed, but it could actually prevent university staff from working with students challenged by their personal relationships. Granted, it may be that the institutions themselves do not support non-heteronormative romantic relationships, but to pretend they do not exist does not only disservice and ignore LGBTQ students, it also limits valuable conversations about this marginalized community, which impacts the staff, faculty, and students working, studying, and living beside them.

six

INTERPRETATIONS
AND IMPACT

I think that we would all agree that it can be good—
great!—to marry someone because you want to be with
them. But what we are talking about is dating someone
because you want marriage, not because you want to
marry that specific person. People might really want
marriage, but they may just have a distaste for the institution of ring by spring. So, it's like if I do it on my own
terms, that's okay, but I'll make fun of ring by spring even
if in the end I ultimately want the same thing. The intention is just slightly nuanced.

A FEW YEARS AGO, I was at a coffee shop grading an assignment
from one of my sociology courses. The coffee shop was close to a
Christian university, a popular spot for students to work and so-
cialize. As I read my students' papers, I was distracted by a table
of young women next to me talking about relationships. Not their
own, but their peers' romantic relationships. I tried not to listen
too closely, but since RxS had already piqued my interest, I sought
to learn more about how students understood it from this particular college environment. After a few minutes of gossip about who
was dating who, and who was about to become engaged, one of the
women shared that she had recently turned down an offer to go to

coffee with a young man, asserting, "I could never marry someone shorter than me!"

My initial thought was, "Oh my goodness, he just asked you to coffee!" and silently judged the girls for taking dating more seriously than I would have advised. "Why not get to know the person better?" I thought, "You two might click!" But as the conversation continued, their comments grew very serious. It became clear that they understood dating to mean pre-engagement, and that God was going to make it clear whom they should marry based on the desires of their hearts.[1] They expected this clarity to come even before the courtship process began. They shared with each other the disappointment they felt when the men they were interested in began dating someone else, and the emotions this evoked. They expressed concern that all of the men at their school who were marriage material were already in relationships, and how they were afraid that they would be single for life. One of the girls spoke about her parents sharing these concerns. She mentioned that she was anxious to go home for Christmas to have to admit to her friends, family, and church that she was still single. I could sense the sadness, shame, and stress in her tone. Then one of the young women said something that struck me to the core. She said, "I feel so unworthy and unwanted. I am so afraid I'm going to be alone forever."[2]

Unworthy. Pressure. Shame. Insecurity. This comment, along with other student reflections, indicates that the pressure that results from RxS is not trivial. It has an intense impact on students and graduates of Christian colleges. Even if students do not wish to marry before graduation, they are nonetheless subject to the culture that encompasses campus life. Joking about finding a spouse is not benign. Joking about it can strike an individual at their core, resulting in unwarranted feelings of worthlessness, inferiority, and fear.

1. A common phrase, coming from the Bible in Ps 37:4, "Take delight in the Lord, and he will give you the desires of your heart."

2. One of these young women later learned about my study, approached me, and authorized my use of this conversation as an example.

Singleness

Perhaps the most obvious message embedded in the RxS ethos is the normality of marriage or romantic relationships in general. Indeed, marriage can be a wonderful decision for many people. It is considered a sacrament in the Christian tradition, as it represents the unbreakable bond between Christ and the church. It is a sacred relationship when two people become one. Marriage is worthy of celebration and, under the right circumstances, advances the Kingdom and brings more glory to God.

However, marriage is not the only relationship status celebrated in scripture. Singleness is often overlooked and undervalued in Christian communities, despite being presented as a valid option in scripture. Singleness is a gift that is a viable alternative to marriage. In his letter to the Corinthians, Paul affirms that many are called to live out singleness in place of marriage, and that it is equally as righteous in the eyes of God. Yet rarely is the single life celebrated or encouraged in Christian circles. The apostle Paul writes to the church in Corinth, "I wish that all men were as I am. But each man has his own gift from God; one has this gift, another has that. Now to the unmarried and the widows I say: It is good for them to stay unmarried, as I am."[3] Moreover, in 1 Cor 7:32-35 Paul lists the potential benefits of remaining single. The Message paraphrases this passage:

> I want you to live as free of complications as possible. When you're unmarried, you're free to concentrate on simply pleasing the Master. Marriage involves you in all the nuts and bolts of domestic life and in wanting to please your spouse, leading to so many more demands on your attention. The time and energy that married people spend on caring for and nurturing each other, the unmarried can spend in becoming whole and holy instruments of God. I'm trying to be helpful and make it as easy as possible for you, not make things harder. All I want is for you to be able to develop a way of life in which

3. 1 Cor 7:7-8, NRSV.

you can spend plenty of time together with the Master without a lot of distractions.[4]

Recall the research from chapter 2 that explains how and why Christian students may feel pressure to find a spouse in the first place. The fact that the more frequently students attend church corresponds with the increase in pressure to marry indicates that the messages our students are hearing in their church communities are inadequate, if not harmful. What message does the church send to the single adults sitting in the congregation? That a person is incomplete until they find a partner? That singles groups and women and men's retreats are so are often focused on marriages relays the message that singleness just isn't an option? What about church community groups? Why are singles groups only meant to be meet-markets? Why do family-focused ministries exclude individuals who do not have a partner or children?

Even if the church does not intend to discredit singles, the centrality of marriage and invisibility of singleness erases the experiences of single adults all together. Thus, the impact on those who may not fit the dominant narrative of what a family looks like may feel institutionally disenfranchised from the congregation. The only possible solution is to uproot the system, or get married. One student, frustrated with this assumption, contended:

> The acceptance or rejection of ring by spring is built on the question of whether you feel you need to find someone in the next four years. All that I hear from Christians is based on the assumption that I need to find someone! We hear rhetoric in the Christian church that you need to be married, and there is the message that once you get into college, that's where you start to get serious about dating.

Indeed, not only are some Christian communities failing to celebrate or encourage singlehood, it is often dismissed as a temporal state[5] as though singlehood is not an option for adult

4. 1 Cor 7:32-35, The Message.
5. See chapter 4.

Christians. I remember hearing about a church that marketed their single's group to anyone "after high school, but before kids." Thus, single adults who have never married are invisible in some church communities, not having a clear point of connection inside the church. This sends the message to young adults that singleness in mature adulthood is unusual or unacceptable.

While Christian churches may bypass the dating conversation almost entirely when it relates to post-college adults, high school and junior high school church youth groups will often talk about dating or sex (or, more accurately, abstinence), but those conversations end once these teens and young adults enter college. This implies that the Christian community seems to assume that once a student graduates from high school and enters college, he or she is expected to become married. Then, students can graduate and be integrated by participating in family centered activities alive and well in most congregations.

For some single Christians, the message they internalized about being single is that it is abnormal at best, and ungodly at worst. According to one student:

> Part of the problem with the Christian Church is that we are struggling to celebrate singleness! And I think there are attempts to do that, but there is no follow-up. I mean, why can't we have a single's group that isn't a meet-market? When they say "single's group," what they really mean is, "People desiring not to be single." I'm not trying to become a monk or a nun! Come on!

Lack of a dating culture may have long-term consequences. In the traditional undergraduate context, most college students are aged eighteen to twenty-four, formative years in identity development and in establishing important social connections. Without the experiences of dating, students may be denied an important and formative step in the maturation process that prepares them for future relationships: romantic relationships and friendships, even professional relationships with members of different gender groups. Unfortunately, this study is limited to data reported by students in college, or reflecting back on their college experience.

Longitudinal data could provide evidence for or against the hypothesis that RxS impacts relational health post-college. Nonetheless, the pressure to become engaged during college does appear to have a negative impact on some students in the short and long term.

Reaction

Students do not—and cannot—pretend that RxS doesn't exist; they are acutely aware of it, and often criticize others who participate in the culture. Despite the alleged disdain for the term, and the jokes that make it appear humorous, the reality is that RxS is so pervasive that even those students who move against the culture can be negatively impacted. Frustrated with this dynamic, some students at Christian colleges may completely reject dating in order to avoid the unrelenting pressure that comes with pursuing another person romantically.

In my research with current students, I learned that the culture of RxS may actually *deter* students from dating altogether, let alone becoming engaged. Below I describe some of the ways students respond to the RxS culture, even if they do not subscribe to its message.

> It is funny listening to others talk about ring by spring in various aspects of our college's culture, but I think the pressure can also affect us in the opposite way. If you're a typical student, then it might pressure you to fall into marriage or get a ring by spring. But for me, and maybe others, I push back. I have this question sometimes like, "If it wasn't for ring by spring, and me not wanting to be a part of that stereotype, would I have proposed to my girlfriend by now?" You know, "To heck to what everybody thinks." If I didn't have that social pressure, maybe I would have. So am I being pressured to, or pressured against, I don't know. How would I have handled this situation differently if this pressure were not here, and I didn't actively try avoiding being just another statistic?

Some students were so reactive to the RxS phrase that they admitted to altering their dating behaviors just to be sure that they are not pigeonholed as a "ring by spring couple." Individuals may reject dating other students, or couples may avoid becoming engaged to their partner altogether, in order to avoid the threat of being typecast. One student who was engaged in the spring of her senior year kept telling everyone that she and her fiancé were not a RxS couple, despite the fact that their relationship history fit neatly into the category. She commented, "People don't want to fall into that box. I think it is human nature to want to react against that."

Still others gossip about those headed toward engagement as "others," as if they refuse to claim ownership of the phrase, even if their Christian college relationship ends in engagement in their senior year. One student, observing this disassociation, reflected:

> I definitely look outward. I mean, I look at some couples and think, "That couple is definitely a ring by spring couple." I don't know anyone that would actually self-identify that way saying, "Yep, I am ring by spring. I am following that horribly negative thing."

Some students want to get married, yet when they become engaged, some may reject being associated with the engagement culture on campus. Optimal distinctiveness is a concept in the field of social psychology, and it explains that most members in modern, western societies (like the US) want to feel equally accepted and equally unique. Essentially, we desire both social inclusion and individuality. It is a contradiction, yet it is the space that most of us occupy when navigating our social identities. Too much similarity de-individualizes us, and too much adherence to norms propels us into becoming social stereotypes, and since the stereotype around Christian college engagements is perceptibly negative, then dissociation seems like the natural response. In the words of another student:

> I think people know when they are falling into the stereotype. I mean, my friend came back and said, [humorously], "Yep, got the ring by spring!" She like knew that it was happening and owning it, and I don't think people

are ignorant of that. I just don't think they are allowed
to enjoy it. . . . It's like you're damned if you do [get the
ring], and damned if you don't.

It seems that students cannot succeed in this culture. If they
do not find a spouse during their college years, then they are some-
how failing at fulfilling the cultural expectations of attending a
Christian college or university. On the other hand, if they do meet
their future spouse and begin to plan an engagement, their peers
typecast them.

But does every student engagement fit the RxS stereotype?
Are there exceptions? For example, are there non-Christian students who marry for financial reasons, or are there students who
are not rushing to marry for sex or for the allure of a big wedding?
In these cases, would we classify these Christian college students as
distinctive from the RxS culture? I would argue that no, we cannot
separate the different types of engagements because ultimately they
are products of the Christian college environment. As described in
chapter 2, any relationship formed in these environments, whether
or not it was promoted by the institution, is surrounded by cultural
pressures that influence all relationships.

A Cautionary Tale

Cristina and Geoff had been dating for two years at Typical Evangelical Christian University. They were both committed evangelical Christians, both were humanities majors, and both were eager
to get married. In between their junior and senior years, between
the two of them, Cristina and Geoff were invited to participate in
half a dozen weddings. Cristina mentioned this to her academic
advisor who reminded her that Cristina and Geoff did not *need*
a wedding in order to be married. Resistant to the RxS culture,
which advertised engagements with staged photos on social media, boasted big fancy weddings with nearly everyone from school,
and resulted in plenty of debt, the couple talked about how they
could avoid being seen as the stereotypical RxS couple. Instead of

burdening their friends with another wedding to attend, another gift to buy, and another forgettable and clichéd ceremony, the two went to the city courthouse and married with a justice of the peace and a passer-by as their witness.

Cristina and Geoff's first public appearance as husband and wife was at a friend's wedding that following weekend. When asked why they eloped, they joked about wanting an apartment together and their school did not permit cohabitation between students. In reality, however, they were always a bit edgy among their peers. They did not like to do things in standard fashion, so eloping was not only a way to avoid being labeled as "typical," but they did so to still attract attention from their peers.

Cristina found out she was pregnant soon after graduation. This was going to put a damper on her career. She had planned to start a doctoral program in English the following year while Geoff studied for the LSAT and applied to law schools. Geoff was thrilled that Cristina was pregnant, believing that this would mean Cristina would stay home and raise the family, therefore making his schooling the priority. Committed to continuing with graduate school, Cristina chose to accept a program close to her parents, without consulting Geoff, so that they would help them raise the baby. Not only did Geoff not get along with her parents (they were miffed after discovering they had eloped without having invited the family), but there were no law school programs anywhere near their new city of residence. Rather than bringing the two closer together, the new baby seemed to elucidate all of the communication problems Geoff and Cristina shared in their marriage: expectations about gender roles, career ambitions, whether children were in their future, where they would live, and so on.

Cristina and Geoff's marriage survived for only one more year. Their resentment toward each other grew until they were stubbornly unwilling to support the goals and interests of the other person. Despite their separation, they stayed married out of fear of the label "divorced." Meanwhile, Geoff dated a number of women, and Cristian moved back in with her parents who were helping raise their baby. Their divorce was not officially announced until five years after their actual separation. Years later, Cristina has primary custody of their child, and both remain single.

Proceed with Caution

Divorce rates among Christians are equitable with national divorce rates[6] indicating that each marriage is just as fragile as the next, regardless of whether the couple identifies as Christian. Sometimes a relationship fails to thrive because of a difference in personalities, goals, or objectives, not necessarily because one person in the relationship is problematic. Take Cristina and Geoff's story, for example. The two seemed like a good match in college: they shared the same friends, had the same major, both were committed Christians. However, when the reality of life circumstances hit (children, careers, places of residence), their marriage dissipated. They did not communicate their concerns prior to marriage, properly discuss expectations, or develop a long-term plan that they could both agree on. Instead, they continued to make rash decisions without acknowledging how those decisions would affect their partner. Moreover, from the beginning of their marriage they did not invite family and close friends into their relationship as a source of support. The word of caution is, therefore, that all marriages—regardless of age or religion—require basic relationship components prior to saying "I do." Communication, a strong external support base, and adequate emotional and spiritual preparation are a part of this process.

So far, I have suggested that the RxS culture can lead to a number of detrimental situations. This includes creating unnecessary pressure on young women (and sometimes men) to marry during college, stigmatizing single people, stereotyping RxS couples, and even leading people to reject dating, resulting in a delay of romantic relationships all together. What I have yet to explain, however, is how the proponents of the RxS culture may seriously impact young men and women by encouraging unhealthy

6. Stetzer, "Marriage"

relationships, driven by a fear of singleness or a fear of not meeting cultural expectations.

In the RxS context—where romantic relationships are taken seriously very quickly—dating becomes an extremely high-risk activity. A number of alumni, both men and women, offered alternative perspectives on how the pressure to take relationships too far too soon can lead some people into unhealthy relationships. For example, one alumni wrote:

> One of my roommates was so desperate to get married that she was willing to settle for a not-very-nice guy and buy her own engagement ring, just to make sure she was engaged before she graduated.

Here is a story of a young woman so desperate to solidify the relationship that she forced the engagement. Another alum reported:

> The environment that spurred on the ring by spring culture caused me to accept toxic and abusive relationships I feel I would have not accepted without that social pressure, just so I could find a partner and fit in.

"Toxic." The word means poisonous; that it could cause death or illness if internalized. Mental health professionals define toxic relationships as those where conflict is present, where one partner seeks to undermine the other, where there's competition, where there's disrespect and a lack of cohesiveness. All are mentally, emotionally, and/or physically damaging to one or both in the relationship. Unhealthy relationships can result in serious harm emotionally and even physically. The message is unclear about how one is supposed to escape a relationship if the dominant culture expects all relationships to lead to marriage. How is a person supposed to see the backstage of his or her partner unless they are dating?

Another alum also used the term "toxic" to describe his relationship, claiming that if it were not for RxS, he would have left the relationships earlier. As it was, his friends pressured him to continue, leading to an unhealthy situation, but establishing a precedent for him that involved staying with someone, even marrying them, just because dating was only acceptable if the result was engagement.

Toxic relationships are not necessarily the result of one or two emotionally unstable individuals. Toxic relationships may just be the result of conflicting personalities, an unequal partnership, unclear expectations, or immaturity. What is particularly concerning, however, is that some Christians will look for another "Christian" to marry, and use that label as a sufficient measure of one's morality or character, and assume they are a match. Therefore, relationships emerge despite the very real differences between the individuals.

Not all relationships that emerge in the RxS high pressure context are unhealthy or toxic, however. Similarly, not all young marriages or quick engagements are poor decisions. Rather, the combination of the pressure to rush, the sense of desperation, satisficing, and the potentially low standards of finding a mate (i.e., "Christian" being the only standard), can potentially lead to a relationship built on the desire to marry for the sake of marriage, rather than for goodness-of-fit with your partner.

Caveats

There are a few important caveats that are worthy of mention here. First, some students take marriage very seriously, and choose to court or date-to-marry apart from any pre-set cultural expectations. An important part of this research is to demonstrate that while students do encounter pressures to marry, there are also many students who become engaged or marry during college simply because the timing was right. Therefore, discouraging Christian couples from dating or becoming engaged all together could be thwarting strong, healthy marriages. One Christian college graduate writes:

> I was engaged at graduation after four years of dating my high school sweetheart. It was a natural time to become engaged. We talked about waiting until after college to plan a wedding due to the time commitment. It was exciting for us because we had waited a long time for this

part of our relationship, but not necessarily because we
felt an expectation. I was hoping that people didn't think
we got engaged because of a cultural expectation.

Second, not all students at Christian colleges are Christian
and so not all students are affected by the same outside social
forces driving the RxS movement (e.g., religion, traditional family
values, gendered expectations). Nonetheless, the culture remains
dominant and infiltrates the casual relationships from couples
that are not interested in pursuing something serious immediately. Even if the couple does not subscribe to traditional Christian
ideals, they are nonetheless influenced by the RxS mentality that
pervades Christian college campuses.

Take David, for example; a sophomore man at a Christian
college who was a nominal Christian, but was not particularly active in his faith. He wanted to ask Maria, one of his classmates,
out to coffee. They met the following weekend for about an hour.
David was happy to get to know Maria a bit better, but did not feel
that he wanted to pursue anything further with her, romantically.
After a week or so, David started getting dirty looks from Maria's
friends, one of whom was Lori. David and Lori had become friends
earlier that year but now, she had decided to no longer talk with
him because of the way he treated Maria, implying some foul play
was involved for not asking her on another date. Other men on his
dorm floor started teasing him and calling him a "heartbreaker"
for leading Maria into a relationship and then dropping her without having a conversation about it. David then chose not to date or
even pursue friendships with any other women on campus while
he was in college. Consequently, it took David years after graduation to find the confidence and the courage to ask another woman
out to coffee.

On the other hand, take Tonya. A junior transfer student from
a community college who chose to finish at a Christian college
for its reputable business program. Upon arrival, she met Loren
who was also a business major. They connected during their first
class project together and began dating by the end of the term. A
year and a half later, months before graduation, Loren's roommate

became engaged to his college girlfriend and reminded Loren that he only had a few more months to finalize his relationship with Tonya. Because of this conversation and peer pressure from his roommates, Loren asked Tonya to marry him during spring break. Tonya, focused on her summer internship in San Francisco before pursuing her MBA out of state in California, was stunned at the proposal. Tonya knew that Loren was planning on moving to Denver to become a partner at a family owned business. Unprepared to answer Loren, and surprised at his audacity to ask her to give up on her professional goals, she declined, but did not wish to end the relationship. Loren was so taken aback, frustrated, and humiliated, that their relationship ended, leaving both of them sad, confused, and alone.

Finally, consider the case of Jamie, a pre-med student with dreams of working for an international humanitarian medical response organization. She struggled a bit with her first chemistry class and ended up talking to Haley, her resident advisor in her dorm. Haley informed Jamie that it was unusual to have women in the pre-med track at their college. Haley asked whether Jamie had considered nursing instead. "After all," Haley added, "You will probably meet your spouse here, and medical school is difficult to manage with a family." Having been socialized to accept the advice of people she considered her superiors, Jamie consented and became a nursing major. She also met a man between her junior and senior year that she married after graduation. Jamie is thriving in her position as a nurse, but not without questioning her career choice based on the personal opinion of a peer, guided by the RxS ethos.

In each of the above cases, students' romantic lives were shaped or influenced by RxS ethos, even if they did not personally subscribe to the ideology. As explored in previous chapters, religion, parents, peer networks, the college environment, and broader social dynamics are all contributing factors that perpetuate RxS on Christian college campuses. Regardless of the origin of the culture, or the perpetuators of it, leaders at these schools ought to recognize and address the impact that RxS has on its students.

For in the cases described above, both personal and professional consequences came from a misunderstanding of how and when to address engagement on campus.

Lasting Impact

What is ring by spring really about then? Sexual pressure? Fear of singleness? Social identity exploration? Emotional or financial security? Relational satisficing? I argue it can be any or all of these things. What makes matters more complicated is that whether or not students want to be married, the Christian college context is such that it becomes difficult to ignore it. Christian or non-Christian, the intent and impact on students' emotional and social well-being are real. While some universities endorse RxS more than others, the fact remains that the pressure to marry, and the feelings of unworthiness, fear, and doubt, are nonetheless products of the Christian college culture.

Even if Christian colleges intentionally move away from the promotion of marriage ideals, peer groups and religious influences will nonetheless allow the RxS culture to permeate student life. Even though RxS is a running joke on campus, the reality of it stings when a student realizes that he or she actually desires a serious relationship, something that has been taken as preposterous, even laughable. Even though the intent of RxS is meant to be positive, well-intended, and playful, its impact is hardly playful at all.

seven

EQUIPPED

I am intrigued by the idea of being single and free to explore the world for my whole life. That said, I plan to get married eventually because the bond of love intrigues me more.

WHEN I INITIATED MY research on ring by spring in the fall of 2014, a number of students—mostly women—approached me with questions and concerns about their own dating experiences. I was not sure they were aware that I failed at the RxS relationship game, so I was surprised to receive so many email requests for meetings. I assumed that because students knew I was researching RxS that my office was becoming a space for students to share their stories. I anticipated conversations about upcoming engagements and dating advice, but these conversations went in the opposite direction. After the first few student meetings, I realized that each of these students felt like outsiders to the RxS culture. They wanted to meet with me to ask advice about singleness, dating after college, whether they *should* consider marriage at some point, graduate school, careers, etc. They were starving for information that contradicted the college-marriage-family norm that pervaded campus culture. They were lost, and they could not see a way out or even know an alternative life plan could exist.

With this in mind, I began to welcome student conversations about the impact of RxS. Student meetings quickly became regular occurrences in my professional space. I was invited to dormitories to present on my research. Other students needing or wanting to talk were referred to me. I even received a few emails from individuals around the country that heard about my research and wanted to share, or were eager to learn more. All of the conversations allowed students and former Christian college students to share their frustrations or fears without feeling judged for wanting to be engaged or married, despite the stereotype.

While the culture of RxS may seem like a minor issue to those unfamiliar with Christian higher education, allow me to assure you that this relationship pressure is real and powerful and is ubiquitous on Christian college campuses. According to my study, 84 percent of student respondents report that they hear conversations about RxS at least occasionally, and 24 percent say the topic comes up often on campus. As previously reported, there isn't just one person, office, or institution to blame for this pressure; rather, it is the intersection of family, religion, gender, peer relationships, and society at large that instigate these expectations for men and women. Despite the fact that RxS is often a topic of discussion, it is only addressed casually, even whimsically, and fails to address the depth of impact that RxS has on students.

Regardless of the cause or the catalyst behind the culture, those working with Christian college students ought to confront RxS directly. Not necessarily with the intention to discourage young people from finding their mate—on the contrary, I argue that college could be, for some, a perfect place and time to meet a spouse—rather, to address the looming pressures that haunt the dating world at Christian colleges. Students need to be fully aware of the consequences of their decisions. For some, engagement and marriage may be perfectly timed during college, others may settle in relationships too soon, or before they are emotionally, financially, or spiritually prepared.

Marital Preparedness

Traditional college students represent a range of maturity levels and life experiences. Thus, the concept of marriage itself has different sociocultural meanings to different people, just as dating and marriage has meant different things in various times and spatial contexts. The notion that a twenty-two-year-old man or woman would be unprepared for marriage would have been ludicrous a century ago. Women and men were less likely to attend college to prepare them for a career, career options were fewer, and women's options were even fewer still, so relying on a husband to provide for her was the norm. People were starting families at a much earlier age and having more children than they are having today. Thus, it made sense to marry to start the next phase of life for both financial and familial reasons.

As discussed previously, developmental psychologists contend that emerging adults are still constructing their social identities. Emerging adults are in the exploratory process of decision-making, and thus, they may not yet be developmentally ready to make important life decisions such as major selection or mate selection without a structured period of self-reflection, learning, and growth.[1] Moreover, college students have—for the most part—not reached *identity achievement*, a term that implies that an individual identity status remains constant following a crisis, in which a sense of commitment to family, work, and religious values is established. Unless students have reached this stage, it may be difficult—if not developmentally improbable—for these emerging adults to understand themselves entirely. Studies have found that individuals (eighteen to twenty-four years old) who have achieved identity reported the most genuine intimate relationships. Conversely, those who were characterized as identity confused were the least intimate.[2] As a result, committing to marriage to someone in a similar developmental stage has consequences for the future marriage.

1. Freedman, "Developmental Disconnect."
2. Seiffge-Krenke and Beyers, "Was Erikson Right After All?"

Does this mean that all intimate relationships formed in college are ultimately too disingenuous to be pursued? Absolutely not. The evidence does suggest, however, that the pursuit of long-lasting serious relationships may not be developmentally appropriate for a portion of the college-aged population who have yet to reach significant identity-defining milestones. Thus, the encouragement to meet one's spouse and marry in one's early twenties is not only counter-cultural to broad North American marriage trends (see chapter 2), it also contradicts research in developmental psychology, which presumes that personal and social identities now develop more fully after age twenty-four.

This does not mean that all relationships formed in this period are insignificant; on the contrary, the relationships that are developed during one's twenties will set them up for relationships in their thirties and beyond.[3] Psychologist Meg Jay has written about twenty-something adults today in her book, *The Defining Decade*. She argues that establishing identity capital, making weak ties (social capital), and picking your family are incredibly important things to prepare for during a person's twenties. In reference to the significance of "picking your family," she writes:

> Today, we see marriage as a commitment between two individuals. Western culture is generally individualistic, prizing independence and self-fulfillment in almost all areas. We emphasize rights over duties and choice over obligation. This extends especially to marriage. With some notable exceptions, there has never been more freedom to decide whether, when, and how to partner, and with whom. There is no question that this has led to countless happy unions, as well as the experience of owning one of the most important decisions of our lives. At the same time, the foregrounding of the individual in relationships has caused us to forget about one of our greatest twentysomething opportunities: picking and creating our families.[4]

3. Jay, *Defining Decade*.
4. Jay, *Defining Decade*, 74

The point is to see the long-term implications of even short-term relationships during emerging and early adulthood. Typically, a number of significant factors must align in order to prepare a person for a long-term commitment, including financial independence, completion of education, etc. However, the new emerging adults may not have achieved each life task by the time they graduate college. Given the research on emerging adulthood and the impact of college socialization and individual identities, how prepared can college students actually be for long-term committed relationships or marriage? How prepared are they for the next step?

Marital Preparedness

In my second wave of research, I collected cross-sectional data[5] from students who were engaged and/or married in the spring of 2015. I asked these students to respond to a series of questions in a twenty-one item survey that examined pre-marital preparedness of engaged students. Only one person from each couple participated in the survey to prevent overlap. All couples were in heterosexual male-female relationships. Of the valid responses, 39 percent of survey participants were pre-engaged, 36 percent were engaged, and 25 percent were married. A total of 35 percent of respondents were confident that they were prepared to marry.

The results concluded that only about 35.7 percent of students felt confident that they were prepared to marry, while 28.6 percent felt that they "probably" ready. That means that 36.7 percent of students do not feel prepared to be married (see Figure 7.1). While this is only one-third of the population polled, it is still less than ideal. Ideally, 100 percent of engaged students polled should feel completely confident in such a big decision. If a person feels that they are unprepared to marry, perhaps some additional support ought to be offered or suggested to them.

---

5. Data from a portion of the population at a specific moment in time.

Figure 7.1 Percentage of Engaged Students Feeling Prepared to Marry

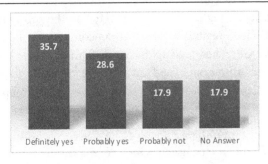

There is a plethora of resources for marital preparation from both a Christian and a secular perspective, ranging from pre-marital counseling with pastors and marriage and family therapists, to books and quizzes to review with your mate, to online programs like PREPARE-ENRICH© or even flash cards from Gottman Institute, there are many inexpensive and available options. Even so, how many Christian college students seek out these materials?

Among the couples in my survey, only 43 percent were enrolled in pre-marital counseling, and only 20 percent had purchased marital preparation books or materials. About half of students (48 percent) report having enrolled in pre-marital counseling, or plan to be enrolled before they marry.[6] This means that almost half of the students at this school at this time are *not* receiving any formal mentoring or guidance prior to saying their vows. It is clear that more guidance is required to better equip students for a lifetime commitment to another person. Being aware of a few resources can help direct students in the right direction. This will be beneficial to them in the long run.

6. Premarital counseling was defined as formal counseling, mentorship, or pre-marital counseling resources (i.e., books)

Unmarried

Another way we can support our students is to encourage them to embrace being single, whether it be for the short term or long term. As mentioned previously, the Christian community often idolizes marriage. Churches tend to focus on family centered activities and outreach programs, and single people remain mostly invisible. There are the occasional "twenty-somethings" groups for the unmarried. One of the students in the focus groups commented:

> Why can't we have a single's group with people dedicated to living a monogamous lifestyle as a choice, and that is something that can bring happiness and fulfillment? That's how you can still have community without feeling isolated or incomplete.

Being unmarried, as opposed to being single, focuses on what an individual is not: married. Singleness on the other hand, indicates an entirely different state of being. Unfortunately, being single is often presented by the Christian community as a struggle one has to bear. One student shared his frustrations in the focus group claiming:

> Singleness in the church is a pejorative term. I feel like everyone wants to ask me, "Why aren't you dating?" There's always the question of "what's wrong with you?"

Kutter Callaway, author of *Breaking the Marriage Idol*, addresses this issue, critiquing the normative model and arguing for a more robust conversation about marriage and singleness in the twenty-first century. He writes that singleness is "a kind of extended purgatory. At best, it is a time of sexual purification that one must endure or suffer through. At worst, celibate singleness is understood to be simply impossible."[7]

It is possible that the church's glorification of traditional marriage and family values sends the message to its followers that a person has not reached his or her full potential until they have reached the sacrament of marriage? A clear hierarchy permeates

7. Callaway, *Breaking the Marriage Idol*, 78.

Christian culture, and it is not absent from Christian campuses either. Married or engaged students do, for the most part, carry a higher social status than their single classmates. Reflecting on this, one student said,

> Monks and nuns are up here [holds hand above head], then married Christians [hand at head], then single Christians [hand at waist]. There is a definite hierarchy. And who wants to be at the bottom?

The reality is that some college students do want to marry, but that it is just not happening for them. They want financial partners at age twenty-two, or a travel companion, or want to start families. That is not always a realizable goal; often, students do not meet their spouse in college, and they must make their next life choice as a single individual. This can be very difficult without proper support.

In my conversations with students, I find that I am continually reminding them that their relationship status does not define their worth. That singleness is not a state of purgatory, but a static moment in one's life story. Whether it is temporary or permanent, being single nonetheless prepares a person for relationships of all types. With singleness comes opportunities unavailable to married people. For example, students are free to make their own decisions about where to live/work/travel, it is easier to explore different jobs without feeling like you have to commit to a career for your partner's sake. A single person may have more opportunities to live with friends, or even with family, to save money for a few years. Being single can be an adventure, with its own set of challenges and rewards.

On the opposite side of that coin is recognizing that being single can be difficult, and so dismissing concerns about singleness fails to recognize the deep-seated pain that some students may feel. Being unmarried or single is not the same as being sexually repressed or sexually frustrated. As stated in chapter six, making sex the focus of the conversation for unmarried adults minimizes other issues associated with singleness. Many students who are single—whether by choice or by circumstance—note the challeng-es of being single that extend beyond sexual intimacy. Financial responsibility, for example, is much more manageable with a joint income and joint expenses. Perhaps financial security, then, is a greater concern about being single that should be addressed. One student said:

> Beyond the religious aspect, it's hard to make it on a single income. So if I want to have a family—even adoption—I am going to need a spouse to survive. So I think that just starts to speak to the vast complexities of making single-ness a viable option in this world.

Perhaps instead of focusing our conversations on how to "survive" being a single sexual being, the Christian community could talk about singleness openly and provide encouragement and community to make those individuals feel equally valued into a Christian community or church family.

Furthermore, we need to remember that young twenty-some-things are likely in the developmental stage where experimentation and identity construction is at its peak. While it is certainly pos-sible for a college-aged man or woman to find their mate and begin to make life choices, it is not stated often enough that remaining single is a good option, maybe even a *better* option, for students who are still developing their life goals. Encouraging students to pursue graduate school or to move to the city/state/country that intrigued them will ultimately contribute to the student's personal, professional, and spiritual development.

The Ring by Spring Tradition

Being aware of what students are exposed to outside of formal aca-demic curriculum or residential life activities can help elucidate the ways in which RxS culture is perpetuated on Christian college campuses. There are many cultures and traditions at college that have an important role in fostering a campus community. Tradi-tions may teach students about the history of their institution, promote common values, and create a common connection for alumni and friends of the university. However, traditions can also produce negative results. As one study put it:

> As certain rituals become ingrained in a university's culture, it may become increasingly difficult to recognize the risks that some traditions pose to health and safety, requiring university officials to take appropriate action to correct them. Similarly, as campus populations become increasingly diverse, traditions that fail to create an inclusive environment for historically marginalized students must change as well.[8]

After years of researching the topic, I find it difficult to justify supporting a culture that uses the "ring by spring" tagline as a way of maintaining campus culture. While RxS may be a common tradition that unites students at Christian colleges and universities, I contend that there is sufficient evidence to suggest that the negative output from pushing heterosexual relationships is enough to reform or reject the tradition entirely. True, university staff cannot fully manage student culture, but it is imperative to recognize the faults that come from what may seem like a harmless attempt to make love connections on campus.

Moreover, the ring by spring tag-line mocks a group of young adults who are presumed to be ignorant of dating and courtship norms, and makes light of those convicted by interpretations of scripture that reflect a more conservative perspective of dating, marriage, and sex. These values held by many students on Christian college campuses, not just those with an engagement ring, are valid. Influential people and places (parents, churches, peers, society), have taught many Christian college students that marriage is the norm, marriage is holy, and marriage is a step toward adulthood. However, when students express these desires on campuses, they are reputed to be ignorant of dating and of the challenges marriage holds. Rather than blaming these students for their theological convictions, why not come beside them and offer them the support needed to make the best decisions.

8. Van Jura, "Tradition Today," 107.

Surviving the Ring by Spring Culture

Regardless of whether the pressure to marry in college is perpetuated by the distinct conditions that comprise Christian colleges or not, the reality is that it must be addressed to best serve our students to make them happier, healthier, and more successful adults in life and love. The legacy of RxS may exist primarily on Christian college campuses, but that does not mean its effects on students are limited to the four years that they are on campus. More research is required to look into the long-term impact of RxS on single college graduates. Yet, there is enough data from my research to suggest that promoting a RxS ethos does little to improve the lives of students on college campuses. If students want to date to marry while on campus they should feel free to do so, without any added pressure from Christian colleges or churches.

Throughout this book, I have suggested that RxS is a culture produced by a faction of the Christian college population, perpetuated by decades of first-person stories, institutional time-honored traditions, and religious, familial, and peer influences. Suffice it to say, most Christian colleges themselves produce and reproduce the RxS narrative, even if the message is mostly perpetuated by student peers. I consider it a responsibility, if not a moral obligation, as a faculty member at a Christian college to explicitly address these issues so that we can support our students—single and coupled—as they work their way through the muck and the mire of dating on Christian campuses.

Christian colleges have a variety of resources available to support students who may find themselves at a relationship crossroad. Among these resources are a faculty population of highly educated, successful Christian adults who deeply care about the students in their classes, a well-respected student life center that connects with our students on a personal level every day. Most campuses have an on-campus student health center with trained counselors and health educators that work with students on encouraging healthy lifestyles and promoting self-care. Finally, students have access to spiritual life leaders, available to students seeking guidance through prayer and scripture, and an eager and curious student population directly affected by the RxS culture.

Each of these areas of influence has the potential to provide a cultural toolbox, specific to their unit on campus that can address the impact of RxS to students at different levels. What these groups develop is likely to be unique to the culture and demographic composition of that particular Christian college. The intent of the list below is not to be directive; rather it is suggestions that Christian college students and employees should consider when addressing how RxS affects their campuses.

Encourage those who are dating to date well. Encourage couples to seek out resources (counseling, books, mentors, etc.) to help them feel confident in their future marriage, or to recognize the challenges in their relationship that may need addressed before saying, "I do." Open conversations about alternatives: about career opportunities and about the impact marriage and family has on future economic endeavors.

Alleviate the pressure to be in a relationship by reminding students that they should focus on relationships of all kinds, rather than assuming marriage is the only relationship worthy of attention.

Reject the status afforded to those couples that have reached their marriage potential at age twenty-one or twenty-two. There is nothing inherently superior about one's marital status, so let us stop using rhetoric that implies that marriage is ideal.

Make singleness a viable alternative for students. Being single is a gift, and doesn't have to imply impermanence. There is no guarantee that every Christian person will find their partner. Instead of creating an environment where individuals feel pressured to marry just to fit the culture, let us highlight and model healthy single lifestyles without suggesting that singleness is always a temporary stage of life.

Beware of college traditions, and act when necessary. What is the real purpose for perpetuating the RxS culture on campus? Is maintaining the legacy more important than our student's emotional and spiritual well-being? Acting could be as simple as taking the phrase out of formal institutional documents.

Finally, support students through prayer and positive Christian mentorship. The hallmark criteria for employment at a Christian college is an active Christian faith. Faculty, staff, administrators, clergy, and other employees have the opportunity to help our students develop spiritually, be it through chapels, classroom or office discussions, campus programming, or prayer in private settings. This will not only help Christian students discern their vocations, but it will also provide them with confidence that their decisions are inspired by their faith convictions.

EPILOGUE

THERE ARE MANY GREAT love stories that begin in college. I witnessed many of these journeys unfold before me as an eighteen-year-old freshman at my Christian college. Many of these couples are still thriving, and I believe that their story was the best scenario for their specific relationship. Some of these couples recall moments early in their marriage where one supported the other through graduate school, claiming that without the financial and emotional support of their spouse, they may not have ever survived past the first six months after graduation. I recall stories where newlyweds agreed to commit to the Peace Corps or Wycliffe Bible Translators for the first years of their marriage: an adventure that they never would have had the courage to take on alone. Sometimes the couple is ready to have children, so that becomes the next step and they grow as a family together. All of these stories are beautiful and should be celebrated, but they are not the only stories out there. Not all college marriages resulted in these happy endings.

I enjoyed my years as a student at a Christian college. It inspired me to pursue my doctorate and return to a Christian college campus, so that I could give back to the students in the same way my professors and mentors supported me during those critical years. Now that I am more aware of the complexity of Christian college culture, I feel compelled as a sociologist and as a Christian to be informed and prepared to address the impact of RxS on my campus, and to consider its lasting effect on our students.

This book is not meant to be a comprehensive examination of the RxS culture; rather, it is an initial exploration into the ways students are impacted by this tradition. The many dynamics that comprise the culture are so complex that sociologists, psychologists, theologians, and other social scientists have plenty to explore for deeper analysis. What I have learned from this study is the importance of listening. Listening to students' stories, to what excites them, to what gives them fear and anxiety.

My attempt in this book is to share some of these stories so that others may also be made aware of how the ring by spring piece of Christian college culture—though steeped in tradition, and albeit with good intentions—can be challenging, burdensome, and heartbreaking for some students. With this knowledge, perhaps we can move forward together with stronger individuals, stronger relationships, and establish more amenable places of higher learning for young Christians to study and grow.

DISCUSSION QUESTIONS

Chapter 1

1. If you were raised in the Christian tradition, did your church or youth group talk about romantic relationships? What about managing friendships across gender lines?

2. What is your personal experience with the ring by spring culture?

3. What is your approach to dating in college? What do you think is the best way to prepare yourself for dating, singleness, and marriage?

Scriptural Reflection: Gen 2:22–24 (NRSV)

And the rib that the Lord God had taken from the man he made into a woman and brought her to the man. Then the man said, "This at last is bone of my bones and flesh of my flesh; this one shall be called Woman, for out of Man this one was taken." Therefore a man leaves his father and his mother and clings to his wife, and they become one flesh.

Chapter 2

1. What do you see as the pros/cons of marrying young (before age twenty-four)? What are the pros/cons of marrying later in life (after age twenty-four)?

2. Do you see younger generations challenging the traditional cultural values of older expectations? If so, how? If not, do you think generational views will eventually clash?

3. What do you think is unique about the Christian college that leads to the ring by spring dynamic?

Scriptural Reflection: Luke 20:34–35 (NRSV)

Jesus said to them, "Those who belong to this age marry and are given in marriage; but those who are considered worthy of a place in that age and in the resurrection from the dead neither marry nor are given in marriage.

Chapter 3

1. Do the statistics in this chapter reflect your personal experience or the experiences of others you know who have interacted with ring by spring culture?

2. Do you think religious groups maintain traditional views of marriage? As society becomes more progressive in general, what is the future of Christian dating and marriage?

3. How can a person be true to their values (whether conservative or progressive) and feel comfortable studying, worshipping, and living in an environment where there are so many perspectives about dating and marriage?

Scriptural Reflection: Col 3:1–4 (NRSV)

So if you have been raised with Christ, seek the things that are above, where Christ is, seated at the right hand of God. Set your minds on things that are above, not on things that are on earth, for you have died, and your life is hidden with Christ in God. When Christ who is your life is revealed, then you also will be revealed with him in glory.

Chapter 4

1. Why is ring by spring so different for men and women? How have you seen this play out in your personal life?

2. There is a joke that some women go to Christian colleges seeking their "MRS" (their marriage license). Are there men that go to college looking for a spouse? If so, why don't we hear more about them? If not, why not? Why don't we have similar jokes for men looking for spouses (or do we)?

3. How should Christians view the institution of marriage? Is the social pressure for women to marry outdated?

Scriptural Reflection: Eph 5:21–30, 33 (NRSV)

Be subject to one another out of reverence for Christ. Wives, be subject to your husbands as you are to the Lord. For the husband is the head of the wife just as Christ is the head of the church, the body of which he is the Savior. Just as the church is subject to Christ, so also wives ought to be, in everything, to their husbands.

Husbands, love your wives, just as Christ loved the church and gave himself up for her, in order to make her holy by cleansing her with the washing of water by the word, so as to present the church to himself in splendor, without a spot or wrinkle or anything of the kind—yes, so that she may be holy and without blemish. In the same way, husbands should love their wives as they do their own bodies. He who loves his wife loves himself. For no one ever hates his own body, but he nourishes and tenderly cares for it, just as Christ does for the church, because we are members of his body. . . . Each of you, however, should love his wife as himself, and a wife should respect her husband.

Chapter 5

1. How have you noticed friendships across gender lines influenced by the ring by spring culture?

2. In your experience, are LGBTQ students considered when talking about dating on campus? Are LGBTQ students comfortable talking about dating in your community? Why or why not?

3. How can we support our friends, partners, and others that may be struggling with views on sex and sexuality?

Scriptural Reflection: 1 Cor 7:1–7 (NRSV)

Now concerning the matters about which you wrote: "It is well for a man not to touch a woman." But because of cases of sexual immorality, each man should have his own wife and each woman her own husband. The husband should give to his wife her conjugal rights, and likewise the wife to her husband. For the wife does not have authority over her own body, but the husband does; likewise the husband does not have authority over his own body, but the wife does. Do not deprive one another except perhaps by agreement for a set time, to devote yourselves to prayer, and then come together again, so that Satan may not tempt you because of your lack of self-control. This I say by way of concession, not of command. I wish that all were as I myself am. But each has a particular gift from God, one having one kind and another a different kind.

Chapter 6

1. Do you know anyone who has felt pressured to marry, even if they do not see themselves marrying before they graduate college? How did this pressure affect him or her?

2. What is your reaction to Cristina and Geoff's story? How would you support them if they were your friends?

3. How do you support a friend that may feel that they have fallen short the cultural expectation to become engaged during college?

Scriptural Reflection: 1 Cor 7:25–34 (NRSV)

Now concerning virgins, I have no command of the Lord, but I give my opinion as one who by the Lord's mercy is trustworthy. I think that, in view of the impending crisis, it is well for you to remain as you are. Are you bound to a wife? Do not seek to be free. Are you free from a wife? Do not seek a wife. But if you marry, you do not sin, and if a virgin marries, she does not sin. Yet those who marry will experience distress in this life, and I would spare you that. I mean, brothers and sisters, the appointed time has grown short; from now on, let even those who have wives be as though they had none, and those who mourn as though they were not mourning, and those who rejoice as though they were not rejoicing, and those who buy as though they had no possessions, and those who deal with the world as though they had no dealings with it. For the present form of this world is passing away.

I want you to be free from anxieties. The unmarried man is anxious about the affairs of the Lord, how to please the Lord; but the married man is anxious about the affairs of the world, how to please his wife, and his interests are divided. And the unmarried woman and the virgin are anxious about the affairs of the Lord, so that they may be holy in body and spirit; but the married woman is anxious about the affairs of the world, how to please her husband.

Chapter 7

1. At what point does someone become an adult? That is, what do you think is necessary for someone to reach adulthood? How do you know?

2. How can a person be prepared spiritually, emotionally, and intellectually to enter college? How can the church leaders and Christian mentors better serve emerging adults in their ministries?

3. How can Christian colleges and universities prepare students for singleness, dating, and marriage? How can you help prepare yourself for your current and future relationship statuses?

Scriptural Reflection: Jer 29:11–13 (NRSV)

For surely I know the plans I have for you, says the LORD, plans for your welfare and not for harm, to give you a future with hope. Then when you call upon me and come and pray to me, I will hear you. When you search for me, you will find me; if you seek me with all your heart.

BIBLIOGRAPHY

Adams, Liam. "'Ring by Spring': How Christian Colleges Fuel Students' Rush to Get Engaged." *Chronicle of Higher Education* (November 2017). https://www.chronicle.com/article/Ring-by-Spring-How/241840.

American College Health Association. "National College Health Assessment II: Reference Group Undergraduates Executive Summary." *American College Health Association* (2017).

Anderson, Dianna. *Damaged Goods: New Perspectives on Christian Purity.* New York: Jericho, 2015.

Arnett, Jeffrey J. *Emerging Adulthood: The Winding Road from the Late Teens through the Twenties.* London: Oxford University Press, 2004.

———. "Young People's Conception of the Transition to Adulthood." *Youth and Society* 29 (1997) 3–23.

Arum, Richard, Josipa Roksa, and Michelle J. Budig. "The Romance of Higher Education: College Stratification and Mate Selection." *Research in Social Stratification and Mobility* 26.2 (2008) 107–21.

Aughinbaugh, Alison, Omar Robles, and Hugette Sun. "Marriage and Divorce: Pattern by Gender, Race, and Educational Attainment." *Monthly Labor Review,* US Bureau of Labor Statistics, 2013.

Barber, Jennifer S., and William G. Axim. "Gender Roles, Attitudes, and Marriage Among Young Women." *Sociological Quarterly* 39 (1998) 11–29.

Barich, Rachel Rosemand, and Denise D. Bielby. "Rethinking Marriage: Change and Stability in Expectations, 1967–1994." *Journal of Family Issues* 17 (1996) 139–69.

Barnett, Rosalind Chait, et al. "Planning Ahead: College Seniors' Concerns About Career-Marriage Conflict." *Journal of Vocational Behavior* 62 (2003) 305–19.

Bartkowski John P. *Remaking the Godly Marriage: Gender Negotiation in Evangelical Families.* New Brunswick: Rutgers University Press, 2001.

Bartkowski, John P., Xu Xiaohe, and Kristi M. Fondren. "Faith, Family, and Teen Dating: Examining the Effects of Personal and Household Religiosity on Adolescent Romantic Relationships." *Review of Religious Research* 52.3 (2011) 248–65.

Beck, Julie. "When Are You Really an Adult?" *The Atlantic* (January 2016). https://www.theatlantic.com/health/archive/2016/01/when-are-you-really-an-adult/422487.

Beste, Jennifer. *College Hookup Culture and Christian Ethics*. London: Oxford University Press, 2017.

Bolzendahl, Catherine, et al. "Changing Counts, Counting Change: Americans' Movement toward a More Inclusive Definition of Family." In *Families as They Really Are*, edited by B. Risman and V. Rutter, 84–95. New York: Norton, 2010.

Brimeyer, Ted M., and William L. Smith. "Religion, Race, Social Class, and Gender Differences in Dating and Hooking Up among College Students." *Sociological Spectrum* 32.5 (2012) 462–73.

Brown, Susan L., Wendy D. Manning, and Krista K. Payne. "Two Decades of Stability and Change in Age at First Union Formation." *Journal of Marriage and Family* 76 (2014) 247–60.

Bryant, Alyssa N. "Assessing the Gender Climate of an Evangelical Student Subculture in the United States." *Gender and Education* 18.6 (2006) 613–34.

Burdette, Amy M., et al. "'Hooking Up' at College: Does Religion Make a Difference?" *Journal for the Scientific Study of Religion* 48.3 (2009) 535–51.

Burgess, Katherine. "Looking to Get Married? Try a Christian College." *The Washington Post* (October 11, 2013). https://www.washingtonpost.com/national/on-faith/looking-to-get-married-try-a-christian-college/2013/10/11/ef6fed4c-32b3-11e3-ad00-ec4c6b31cbed_story.html?utm_term=.9ebda82823ee.

Callaway, Kutter. *Breaking the Marriage Idol*. Downers Grove, IL: Intervarsity, 2018.

Carpenter, Laura. "Like a Virgin . . . Again?: Secondary Virginity as an Ongoing Gendered Social Construction." *Sexuality & Culture* 15.2 (2011) 115–40.

Carroll, Jason S., et al. "So Close, Yet So Far Away: The Impact of Varying Marital Horizons on Emerging Adulthood." *Journal of Adolescent Research* 22 (2007) 219–47.

Centers for Disease Control (CDC). "Cohabitation, Marriage, Divorce, and Remarriage in the United States." *Vital and Health Statistics* 23 (July 2002). https://www.cdc.gov/nchs/data/series/sr_23/sr23_022.pdf.

"Changing Attitudes on Gay Marriage." *Pew Research Center Forum* (June 2017). www.pewforum.org/fact-sheet/changing-attitudes-on-gay-marriage/.

Cherlin, Andrew J. "The Deinstitutionalization of American Marriage." *Journal of Marriage and Family* 66.4 (2004) 848–61.

———. *The Marriage Go-Round: The State of Marriage and the Family in America Today*. New York: Vintage, 2009.

Coley, Jonathan. *Gay on God's Campus: Mobilizing for LGBT Equality at Christian Colleges and Universities*. Durham: University of North Carolina Press, 2018

Coontz, Stephanie. *Marriage, a History: How Love Conquered Marriage.* New York: Penguin, 2006.

Council for Christian Colleges and Universities (CCCU). "Advancing Faith and Intellect for the Common Good." October 2018. https://www.cccu.org/about/.

Davis, Shannon N. "Family Ideologies, Religion, and Teen Dating Practices." Paper presented at the American Sociological Association Conference. Montreal, Quebec, Canada, August 2006.

Day, Randal D., and Alan Acock. "Marital Well-Being and Religiousness as Mediated by Relational Virtue and Equality." *Journal of Marriage & Family* 75.1 (2013) 164–77.

Defranza, Megan. *Sex Difference in Christian Theology: Male, Female and Intersex in the Image of God.* Grand Rapids, MI: Eerdmans, 2015.

Diefendorf, Sarah. "After the Wedding Night: Sexual Abstinence and Masculities Over the Life Course." *Gender & Society* 29.5 (2014) 647–69.

Dimock, Michael. "Defining Generations: Where Millennials End and Post-Millennials Begin." *Pew Research Forum,* March 2018. www.pewresearch.org/fact-tank/2018/03/01/defining-generations-where-millennials-end-and-post-millennials-begin/.

Dougherty, Kevin D., Melanie Hulbert, and Ashley Palmer. "Marital Naming Plans among Students at Four Evangelical Colleges. *Religions* 5.4 (2014) 1116–31.

Ducharme, Jamie. "How to Tell if You're In a Toxic Relationship—And What to Do About It." *Time,* June 2018. http://time.com/5274206/toxic-relationship-signs-help/.

Duvall, Evelyn Millis. "Research Finds: Student Marriages." *Marriage and Family Living* 22.1 (1960) 76–77.

Erzen, Tanya. *Straight to Jesus: Sexual and Christian Conversions in the Ex-Gay Movement.* Berkeley: University of California Press, 2006.

Fahs, Breanne. "Daddy's Little Girls." *Frontiers: A Journal of Women Studies* 31.3 (2010) 116–42.

Fileta, Debra K. *True Love Dates: Your Indispensable Guide to Finding the Love of Your Life.* Grand Rapids: Zondervan, 2018.

Freedman, Liz. "The Developmental Disconnect in Choosing a Major: Why Institutions Should Prohibit Choice until Second Year." *The Mentor: An Academic Advising Journal* (June 2013). https://dus.psu.edu/mentor/2013/06/disconnect-choosing-major/.

Freitas, Donna. *Sex and the Soul: Juggling Sexuality, Spirituality, Romance, and Religion on America's College Campuses.* New York: Oxford University Press, 2015.

Gallagher, Sally, and Christian Smith. "Symbolic Traditionalism and Pragmatic Egalitarianism: Contemporary Evangelicals, Families, and Gender." *Gender and Society* 13 (1999) 211–33.

Ganong, Lawrence, and Elizabeth Sharp. "Raising Awareness about Marital Expectations: Are Unrealistic Beliefs Changed by Integrative Teaching?" *National Council on Family Relations* 49 (2000) 71–76.

Garcia, Justin R., et al. "Sexual Hookup Culture: A Review." *Review of General Psychology* 16.2 (2012) 161–76.

Gassanov, Margaret A., Lisa M. Nicholson, and Amanda Koch-Turner. "Expectations to Marry Among American Youth: The Effects of Unwed Fertility, Economic Activity, and Cohabitation." *Youth & Society* 40 (2008) 265–88.

Gay, David A., Christopher G. Ellison, and Daniel A. Powers. "In Search of Denominational Subcultures: Religious Affiliation and 'Pro-Family' Issues Revisited." *Review of Religious Research* 38 (1996) 3–17.

Gehrz, Chris. "Marriage, Friendship, and the Mission of Christian Colleges." *The Pietist Schoolman* (July 2017). https://pietistschoolman.com/2017/07/27/marriage-friendship-and-the-mission-of-christian-colleges.

George, Stacy Keogh. "Beyond the Ring by Spring Culture." *The Institute for Faith and Learning at Baylor University* (2016) 46–54. https://www.baylor.edu/content/services/document.php/277020.pdf.

Goodman, Michael A., et al. "Religious Faith and Transformational Processes in Marriage." *Family Relations* 62.5 (2013) 808–23.

Grant, Jonathan. *Divine Sex: A Compelling Vision for Christian Relationships in a Hypersexualized Age.* Grand Rapids, MI: Brazos, 2015.

Grasmick, Harold G., Linda P. Wilcox, and Sharon K. Bird. "The Effects of Religious Fundamentalism and Religiosity on Preference for Traditional Family Norms." *Sociological Inquiry* 60 (1990) 352–69.

Haer, Kelly Maxwell. "The Difficulty of Defining Relationships." *I Survived, I Kissed Dating Goodbye* (February 2018) https://www.isurvivedikdg.com/single-post/2018/02/01/The-Difficulty-of-Defining-Relationships---Part-I.

Harden, Nathan. "Peter Pan Goes to College." *Society* 50.3 (2013) 257–60.

Harris, Joshua. *I Kissed Dating Goodbye: A New Attitude to Relationships and Romance.* Portland, OR: Multnomah, 2003.

Henig, Robin Maranatz. "What Is It about 20-Somethings?" *New York Times Magazine* (August 2010). https://www.nytimes.com/2010/08/22/magazine/22Adulthood-t.html?pagewanted=1.

Hirsch, Debra. *Redeeming Sex: Naked Conversations about Sexuality and Spirituality.* Downers Grove, IL: Intervarsity, 2015.

Hull, Kathleen E., Ann Meier, and Timothy A. Ortyl. "Young Adult Relationship Values at the Intersection of Gender and Sexuality." *Journal of Marriage and Family* 71 (2009) 510–25.

Hymowitz, Kay, et al. "Knot Yet: The Benefits and Costs of Delayed Marriage in America." *The National Marriage Project* (2013). http://nationalmarriageproject.org/wordpress/wp-content/uploads/2013/04/KnotYet-FinalForWeb-041413.pdf.

Isaac, Susan V., Roger C. Bailey, and Walter L. Isaac. "Perceptions of Religious and Nonreligious Targets Who Participate in Premarital Sex." *Social Behavior & Personality: An International Journal* 23.3 (1995) 229–35.

Jay, Meg. *The Defining Decade: Why Your Twenties Matter and How to Make the Most of Them Now.* New York: Hachette, 2012.

Kelchen, Robert. "Examining Variations in Marriage Rates Across Colleges." *Brookings Institute* (July 2017). https://www.brookings.edu/blog/brown-center-chalkboard/2017/07/17/examining-variations-in-marriage-rates-across-colleges/.

Kelley, H. H., and J. E Thibaut. *Interpersonal Relations: A Theory of Interdependence.* New York: Wiley, 1978.

King, Jason. *Faith with Benefits: Hookup Culture on Catholic Campuses.* New York: Oxford University Press, 2017.

Kingston, P. W., et al. "Why Education Matters." *Sociology of Education* 76 (2003) 53–70.

Koball, Heather L. "Crossing the Threshold: Men's Incomes, Attitudes Toward the Provider Role, and Marital Timing." *Sex Roles* 51 (2004) 387–95.

Kuperberg, Arielle. "Age at Coresidence, Premarital Cohabitation, and Marriage Dissolution: 1985–2009." *Journal of Marriage & Family* 76.2 (2014) 352–69.

Lahad, Kinneret. "Singlehood, Waiting, and the Sociology of Time." *Sociological Forum* 27.1 (2012) 163–86.

Landor, Antoinette, and Leslie Simons. "Why Virginity Pledges Succeed or Fail: The Moderating Effect of Religious Commitment versus Religious Participation." *Journal of Child & Family Studies* 23.6 (2014) 1102–13.

Larson, J. "The Marriage Quiz: College Students' Beliefs in Selected Myths About Marriage." *Family Relations* 37 (1988) 3–11.

Lee, G., and K. Payne. "Changing Marriage Patterns Since 1970: What's Going On, and Why?" *Journal of Comparative Family Studies* 41.4 (2010) 537–55.

Mahay, J., and A. C. Lewin. "Age and the Desire to Marry." *Journal of Family Issues* 28 (2007) 706–23.

Malone, Dana M. *From Single to Serious: Relationships, Gender and Sexuality on American Evangelical Campuses.* New Jersey: Rutgers University Press, 2018.

Mannheim, Karl. "The Problem of Generations." In vol. 5 of *Essays on the Sociology of Knowledge: Collected Works,* edited by Paul Kecskemeti, 276–322. New York: Routledge, 1952.

Manning, Karl. "Loosening the Ties that Bind: Shaping Student Culture." In *Cultural Perspectives in Student Affairs,* edited by G. D. Kuh, 95–109. Lanham, MD: University Press of America, 1993.

Mare, R. D. "Five Decades of Educational Assortative Mating." *American Sociological Review* 56 (1991) 15–32.

Marini, Margaret Mooney. "The Transition to Adulthood: Sex Differences in Educational Attainment and Age at Marriage." *American Sociological Review* 43.4 (1978) 483–507.

Mikkelson, Alan C., Colin Hesse, and Perry M. Pauley. "The Attributes of Relational Maximizers." *Communication Studies* 67.5 (2016) 567–87.

Mikkelson, Alan C., and Perry M. Pauley. "Maximizing Relationship Possibilities: Relational Maximization in Romantic Relationships." *The Journal of Social Psychology* 153 (2013) 467–85.

Miller, Claire Cain, and Quoctrung Bui. "Equality in Marriages Grows, and So Does Class Divide." *New York Times* (February 2016). https://www.nytimes.com/2016/02/23/upshot/rise-in-marriages-of-equals-and-in-division-by-class.html.

Moore, A. K., and M. T. Stief. "Changes in Marriage and Fertility Behavior: Behaviors versus Attitudes of Young Adults." Washington, DC: Child Trends Inc., 1989.

National Center for Education Statistics (NCES). "Data Point: Beginning College Students Who Change Their Majors Within 3 Years of Enrollment." US Department of Education NCES 2018–434 (December 2017).

Novotney, Amy. "Students Under Pressure." *Monitor on Psychology* 45 (2014) 36. www.apa.org/monitor/2014/09/cover-pressure.aspx.

Nunn, Lisa M. "Talking Teens into Abstinence *Making Chastity Sexy: The Rhetoric of Evangelical Abstinence Campaigns* by Christine Gardner." *Journal of Sex Research* 51.7 (2014) 838–39.

Papke, David Ray. "Community Colleges: The Boston Junior College Blues." *Change* 7.5 (1975) 52–53.

Pedersen, Willy. "Forbidden Fruit? A Longitudinal Study of Christianity, Sex, and Marriage." *Journal of Sex Research* 51.5 (2014) 542–50.

Parsons, Talcott, and G. M. Platt. *The American University*. Cambridge: Harvard University Press, 1973.

Pew Research Center. "Religious Landscape Survey: Gender Composition." *Pew Research Center* (2014) http://www.pewforum.org/religious-landscape-study/gender-composition/.

Prior, Karen Swallow. "The Case for Getting Married Young." *The Atlantic* (March 2013). https://www.theatlantic.com/sexes/archive/2013/03/the-case-for-getting-married-young/274293/.

Ravizza, Bridget Burke. "Let's Talk about Sex . . . on Christian College Campuses." *America: The Jesuit Review* (April 2014). https://www.americamagazine.org/arts-culture/2018/04/20/lets-talk-about-sexon-christian-college-campuses.

Regenerus, Mark, and Jeremy Uecker. *Premarital Sex in America: How Young Americans Meet, Mate, and Think about Marrying*. London: Oxford University Press, 2011.

Robertson, Brandan. *Our Witness: The Unheard Stories of LGBT+ Christians*. Eugene, OR: Cascade, 2018.

Schoen, Robert, and Yen-hsin A. Cheng. "Partner Choice and the Differential Retreat from Marriage." *Journal of Marriage and Family* 68 (2006) 1–10.

Schwartz, C. R., and R. D. Mare. "Trends in Educational Assortative Marriage from 1940–2003." *Demography* 42 (2005) 621–46.

Seiffge-Krenke, I., and W. Beyers. "Was Erikson Right After All? Identity, Attachment and Intimacy of Couples in Young Adulthood." *Psychotherapeutic* 61 (2016) 16–21.

Sheets, Nicole. "Let's Kiss Dating Hello." *Christianity Today* (October 2016). https://www.christianitytoday.com/women/2016/october/do-christian-college-students-still-feel-pressured-to-marry.html.

Sprecher, Susan. "Equity and Social Exchange in Dating Couples: Associations with Satisfaction, Commitment, and Stability." *Journal of Marriage and Family* 36.3 (2001) 599–613.

Stetzer, Ed. "Marriage, Divorce, and the Church: What Do the Stats Say, and Can Marriage Be Happy?" *Christianity Today* (February 2014). https://www.christianitytoday.com/edstetzer/2014/february/marriage-divorce-and-body-of-christ-what-do-stats-say-and-c.html.

Stevens, Mitchell L., Elizabeth A. Armstrong, and Richard Arum. "Sieve, Incubator, Temple, Hub: Empirical and Theoretical Advances in the Sociology of Higher Education." *Annual Review of Sociology* 34 (2008) 127–51.

Thibaut, J. W., and H. H. Kelley. *The Social Psychology of Groups*. New York: Wiley, 1959.

US Census Bureau. "Figure MS-2: Median age at first marriage: 1890 to Present." (2011). https://www.census.gov/content/dam/Census/library/visualizations/time-series/demo/families-and-households/ms-2.pdf.

Van Jura, Matthew J. "Tradition Today: How Student Affairs Professionals Can Strengthen and Preserve Campus Traditions." *The Vermont Collection* 31 (2010) 107–16.

Wang, Wendy, and Paul Taylor. "For Millennials, Parenthood Trumps Marriage." *Pew Research Center* (March 2011). www.pewsocialtrends.org/2011/03/09/iii-millennials-attitudes-about-marriage/.

Wheeler, David R. "The LGBT Politics of Christian Colleges." *The Atlantic* (March 2016). https://www.theatlantic.com/education/archive/2016/03/the-lgbt-politics-of-christian-colleges/473373/.

Wilcox, W. Bradford, Mark Chaves, and David Franz. "Focused on the Family? Religious Traditions, Family Discourse, and Pastoral Practice." *Journal for the Scientific Study of Religion* 43.4 (2004) 491–504.

Wilcox, W. Bradford, N. Wolfinger, and C. Stokes. "One Nation, Divided: Culture, Civic Institutions, and the Marriage Divide." *The Future of Children* 25.2 (2015) 111–27.

Willits, Joel. "What Christian College Students Are Saying about Sex . . . It May Surprise You" *Euangelion* (April 2015). www.patheos.com/blogs/euangelion/2015/04/what-christian-college-students-are-saying-about-sex-it-may-surprise-you/.

Witwer, M. "U.S. Men and Women Now Have Highest Mean Age at Marriage in This Century, Census Bureau Finds." *Family Planning Perspectives* 25.4 (1993) 190.

Woody, Jane D., et al. "Adolescent Non-Coital Sexual Activity: Comparisons of Virgins and Non-Virgins." *Journal of Sex Education & Therapy* 4 (2000) 261–68.

Printed in the USA
CPSIA information can be obtained
at www.ICGtesting.com
LVHW100309080224
771279LV00003B/276